Sipho Tibane

Biblical Financial Principles: Spending versus Saving

Sipho Tibane

Biblical Financial Principles: Spending versus Saving

Learn the ways of an ant

Blessed Hope Publishing

Imprint
Any brand names and product names mentioned in this book are subject to trademark, brand or patent protection and are trademarks or registered trademarks of their respective holders. The use of brand names, product names, common names, trade names, product descriptions etc. even without a particular marking in this work is in no way to be construed to mean that such names may be regarded as unrestricted in respect of trademark and brand protection legislation and could thus be used by anyone.

Cover image: www.ingimage.com

Publisher:
Blessed Hope Publishing
is a trademark of
Dodo Books Indian Ocean Ltd. and OmniScriptum S.R.L publishing group

120 High Road, East Finchley, London, N2 9ED, United Kingdom
Str. Armeneasca 28/1, office 1, Chisinau MD-2012, Republic of Moldova, Europe
Printed at: see last page
ISBN: 978-620-4-18767-9

Reverend S J Tibane

Go to the ant, you sluggard; consider its ways and be wise!

Avoiding poor planning that waste your financial and time resources

Biblical Series of Financial Wisdom and Balance

Go to the ant, you sluggard; consider its ways and be wise!

Preventing poor planning that waste your financial and time resources

Dr Reverend SJ Tibane

P.O Box 403

Son Park

1206

tibanesipho57@gmail.com

http://www.tdcf.com

072 503 1115

Doctor Tibane is a founding member of the Fountain Family Bible Church International, White River, Republic of South Africa.

Dedication

I dedicate this book to my fathers, James William Tibane and Phillip Paulos Tibane who both went to be with the Lord in 2018 and in 2021 respectively. Although my spirit has not rested and settled until to date, every time I think of your contribution in our lives, we feel lonely and stranded. Life is surely poorer without your presence in our midst.

We do believe though that you would both love to see the family going forward in spite of your untimely departure.

Biblical Meaning of Ants in Dreams – Interpretation and Meaning

The interpretation of dreams in modern times differs a bit from the analysis of dreams in the Biblical sense.

Modern psychoanalysis brought the most significant changes in the way dreams are analyzed.

Let us first see how the Bible describes the ants and their symbolic meaning and then we will give you additional information about the Biblical interpretation of ants in dreams.

Biblical Meaning of Ants

Ants are insects which live in highly organized colonies of different sizes. Their societies are characterized by strict division of labour between the individuals, evolved communication and even abilities to solve problems.

They resemble a lot to the organization of the human society. They gather their food for their future use. They join forces to create their underground kingdoms.

Every individual in their society has a distinctive role and it plays it with strict obedience. If attacked or under some kind of danger, these animals can be fierce defendants of their colonies. The Bible uses ants as a good example of cooperation, diligence, as well as providing for the future.

They are also an example of devotion, organization, hierarchy, and system. The Bible uses their characteristics as an example to us humans to follow.

Ants are mentioned many times in the Bible. The Bible calls people to learn from the way ants organize and live their lives, as well as their studiousness and diligence. The Bible reminds us not be lazy asking us to be more like the ants.

People are also recommended to follow the ants' example and provide for their future because although ants are considered weak animals, they are careful and responsible, and they store their food for the future.

People can also learn from the ants' perseverance and strength. The Bible reminds us of the accomplishments they achieve, regardless of their size.

Ants can cross over great distances and lift weight much bigger than their size. Because of that, ants can teach us and encourage us to have faith that we are powerful enough to achieve anything we set our mind to.

Biblical meaning of ants in our dreams

Dreaming about ants in general – Because ants are insects with characteristics we should admire and copy, in general, they are a good sign when they appear in our dreams. They could be considered a confirmation that we are on the right path to achieve our goals, and that we are showing great determination and perseverance while doing that.

Ants could also be a reminder to pay more attention to our spending habits, and think more about the future. Ants remind us to begin saving and ensuring our future security.

Ants could also be a sign of hard work and efforts expecting us in the near future, which will pay off immensely, bringing positive changes and opportunities into our lives.

Dreaming about red ants – If you saw red ants in your dream, such dream could represent some warning regarding people from your surroundings. Maybe you have some hidden enemies who wait for their chance to attack you in some way, so use this dream to be prepared for such events and defend yourself in a proper manner.

Dreaming about ants biting you – If you had a dream about ants biting you, that might not be a good sign regarding some of your future affairs. It is usually linked to your private life, but could also be related to your profession. You will need to focus on the problems which might arise, and even consider consulting some of your friends or family members to help you find the solution with joined forces.

This dream warns you to confront your problems as they arise, or you might cause things growing out of proportion and making them more difficult to resolve.

The message of this dream is not to be afraid to face challenges and ask the ones that are close to you to help you if you don't trust your problem – solving abilities.

Dreaming about crushing ants – If you dreamed you were crushing and killing ants that might not be a good sign. This dream might indicate not having your priorities straight and relying on luck in dealing with essential matters.

Maybe you have been procrastinating and feeling lazy about doing some important things, or postponing them and doing something which isn't that significant, but more interesting.

This dream is a wake-up call to set your priorities and begin dealing with the most important issues you have, so you won't end up in a situation where your attitude creates irreparable damage.

Dreaming about ants inside your home – If you had a dream about your home being infested with ants, such dream might not be a good sign, and might refer to you or someone close to you, experiencing some unpleasant situations.

This dream might be a warning to pay attention to some unexpected enemies and gather forces with your loved ones to reject their possible attack successfully.

Dreaming about catching an ant – If you dreamed you were catching ants, such dream is usually a very good sign, and represents good fortune. This means successful outcomes of your current endeavours.

This is also a good sign regarding your financial situations, as it might signify an increase in income or receiving some unexpected gifts.

Dreaming about ants being on your body – If you dreamed about ants crawling over your body, this dream could be a sign of some discomfort you might experience in the near future. For example, you might be asked to do something you dislike, but you won't be able to get away from this task.

On the other side, this dream could be a confirmation of your great abilities to handle your assets and finances.

Dreaming about seeing ants on your bed – If you saw ants on your bed in your dream, such dream might not be a good sign, possibly indicating trouble and difficulties. These issues might concern your private as well as your professional life. This dream prepares you for the possibility of facing these issues and asks you to confront them instead of avoiding them.

You need to be aware that the problems will need to be solved and won't just disappear, so prepare yourself to deal with them in the most efficient way.

If you need help, ask the ones from your closest circle to give it to you.

Dreaming about ants gathering food – If you observed ants collecting their food in your dream, such dream might be a warning regarding your finances and the way you are handling your financial affairs. This dream reminds you to begin paying attention to your spending habits and start saving money because you might seriously jeopardize your future welfare.

Think about the future and try to provide for yourself and loved ones.

Don't waste your money in vain. This dream could also symbolize your fears related to your financial situation and the possible inability to pay off all your debts.

Dreaming about a colony of ants – If you saw large ant colonies in your dream, such dream is usually a good sign, indicating some changes happening soon in your life. These changes might catch you off-guard, but you will benefit immensely from them.

This dream is preparing you for such events, so you should accept and embrace these changes as soon as possible and start collecting the fruits they are bringing into your life.

Dreaming about having ants in your ears – If you dreamed about having ants in your ears, such dream might be a warning about an approaching danger, you can easily avoid. It might also indicate some concerns or obstacles you will need to take care of very gently and with great care.

The difficulties might be related to you or someone you care about very much, and their resolving will ask great patience and caution on your behalf if you don't want to make a wrong move

THERE ABOUT 15 REASONS WHY SAVING IS CRUCIAL IN A FAMILY SETUP

1. Saving reduces economic insecurity. Generally during old age or after the retirement of the head of the family, economic insecurity may arise. Family's income during this period is reduced. If there are no wage earners in the family the problem will become acute. Economic insecurity can also arise from sudden sickness for which the family may be faced with heavy medical expenditure. The psychological effect of feeling of insecurity is very dangerous.

The family can overcome this situation only by saving money. The money which are saved by the family over the years can reduce the economic insecurity of the family till another member of the family starts earning.

2. Saving helps in the period of physical inability. When the wage earners are becoming sick, they are unable to do the work. In working class families, the labourers or the persons who works on daily wage payment basis may not be paid if they do not turn up for work due to some physical inability. In some work, there is no sick leave and "no work no pay" rule is prevalent. Saving will help the family during such periods.

3. Saving is useful during an emergency. Sudden sickness, accidents, natural calamities, death of the earning member, sudden retrenchment from service is different forms of emergencies. During these periods, the family is forced to incur heavy expenditure for meeting the requirement of the family. In case of sudden unemployment of the head of the family, it will have to manage without income till the new employment. Saving plays an important role during these periods for the proper management. Since an emergency can never be anticipated, the only way of preparing to meet them is through saving.

4. Saving is essential to meet the expenditure, forced by the social customs and traditions. Social customs are very strong in India. More money is spent on the occasion of marriage

ceremonies, thread ceremony etc. Some families take loans for meeting these expenditures to maintain their social prestige. These extra expenditures can be easily met through saving.

5. Saving is required for future use. Today's income may be sufficient for today's needs. But there may be increased needs or decreased income in future. Saving enables one to face the future bravely.

6. Saving is useful for children's education, marriage or other family expenditure. Now-a-days, higher education has become a major item of expenditure. For the marriage of the children, a lump sum amount of money is required. This expenditure can be easily met through saving.

7. Saving is required for making big purchases for the family. In modem life, household durable goods are an essential part of the family. Furniture, furnishings, time and energy saving equipment, television, refrigerator, jewellery etc. are the big purchases of the family. Building or purchasing of house, car are also big items of expenditure. A family which saves purposefully can generally make such big purchases.

8. Saving enhances the socio-economic status of the family. A family which saves more can be prompt in payment of bills etc. That family is considered as a wealthy family among the neighbours. It increases the social prestige and forms a good image in the society. Saving helps in gaining power and prestige for the family.

9. Saving is helpful in securing loans from banks and other institutions, because it acts as the security deposits. Saving has much importance in the family financial management.

10. Saving becomes a source of income. All savings kept in the banks, post offices etc. carry interest. Saving money can be invested in some private companies which can give more amount of profits to the family.

11. Saving helps to maintain standard of living for businessmen, agricultural labourers and other persons who have seasonal income.

12. Saving is a very good habit, which can pass from the parents to their children.

13. Saving is required for pleasure trips, sight-seeing, tours during vacation in some families as these tours require more amount of money at a time.

14. Individual savings of the family increase the nations productive power.

15. People save under various, schemes in post-offices, LIC or banks to get income tax exemption.

Every family should save something regularly from their income. Though rich people are capable to save more than the poor, it is also wrong to think that the poor cannot save at all

Biblical Principles for Saving and Investing Your Money (x7)

Most Christians know they should save and invest for retirement or disability. But many find it difficult to adopt a practical theology for managing their money, especially when it comes to saving and investing for a distant and uncertain future.

It is difficult because there are so many perspectives on this topic. Some promote a life of denial, eschewing any luxuries and savings for the sake of the kingdom. Others suggest budgeting, avoiding debt, and regular saving in order to enjoy greater wealth for giving and spending later in life. In the broader culture, the FIRE (Financial Independence/Retire Early) movement emphasizes extreme frugality and saving to be able to retire before age 40.

With all these seemingly inconsistent and conflicting messages, how can you come up with a personal theology of money that balances biblical orthodoxy with practicality in saving and investing for the future?

Here are seven biblical principles that may help.

1. Saving for Future Needs Is Biblical

Some Christians do not save for retirement because they believe it is disobedient (usually quoting Matt. 6:19–20), or they feel guilty about putting money away when others are in such great need. Others believe it is not necessary because God will take care of them (Isa. 46:4). And some would like to save but spend everything they make (Prov. 13:18).

You may be surprised to learn that saving is actually encouraged in the Bible. Scripture condones saving for known, anticipated needs in the future (Gen. 41; Prov. 6:6–11; Prov. 21:5; Prov. 21:20).

You may be surprised to learn that saving is actually encouraged in the Bible.

The Bible teaches that it is possible to wisely save and invest for the future while also being "rich toward God" by "storing up treasures in heaven" (Luke 12:21; Matt. 6:19–21).

2. Saving Honours God and Serves Others

It would be easy to think of saving as a purely selfish activity. That can indeed be the case—we need only read about the rich fool in Luke 12—but it does not have to be.

Saving honours God because it rightly values money as a gift that he has given to us (James 1:16–17). Instead of unplanned, impulsive, or foolish spending, wise saving demonstrates the importance of stewarding his gifts (Luke 12:47–48).

Proper stewardship will put you in a better position to help with important needs as they arise (Eph. 4:28). You can respond more quickly and perhaps in a more significant way (Prov. 3:27). Saving may also allow you to leave an inheritance, blessing your heirs so they can then be a blessing to others (Prov. 13:22).

3. Procrastination Is a Mistake

We all tend to put things off. But by failing to save early, you forfeit one of the most potent financial forces: tax-free compound interest, or earning interest on interest.

Most people don't postpone saving because they think saving is unimportant. Instead, they expect to have more disposable income down the road, or they have more pressing needs that get in the way, including debt payments, low wages, health-care expenses, or the need to save for a child's education. They plan to get to it later on.

But even if things do change down the road, money saved for retirement later has less time to grow (Matt. 25:27), meaning that you end up having to contribute much more to have the same amount if you started today.

Just start by doing what you can and gain momentum over time.

4. Debt Is Debilitating

The Bible isn't silent about debt. There obviously were not Visa cards or auto loans in Jesus's time, but lending and borrowing were part of the economic landscape. The Bible does not strictly prohibit debt, but it does characterize debt as a form of bondage (Prov. 22:7).

Beyond that, there is a direct correlation between over-spending and too much debt and a low savings rate. In the context of saving, debt comes at a cost. The money needed to service debt, which goes to creditors, is money that can't be used for anything else. That is the "opportunity cost" of debt. Compare borrowing $1,000 and paying 12 percent interest ($120) versus saving $1,000 and investing it at 6 percent ($60). The real economic benefit is 18 percent ($180)!

5. Wise Investing Is Right and Good

Investing is not stock trading. It is not about betting the farm on a hot tip from your brother-in-law. Such speculating amounts to gambling on future events, and most of the time you lose more than you gain (Prov. 28:19; 1 Tim. 6:10).

Investing is actually commended if done wisely. It's about putting money into real businesses that employ people and deliver products or services to customers. Hopefully, the companies we invest in do well and provide a return commensurate with our investment (Prov. 31:10–31; Eccl. 11:1–6).

Most of us would do well to invest in low-cost, passively managed, mutual and exchange-traded index funds (ETFs) instead of individual stocks and bonds. We also need to keep an eye out for high fees and expenses (they can be a big drag on returns), not being diversified enough (assets that balance each other), buying and selling at the wrong time (due to emotion), and a lack of knowledge about your investments (don't buy what you don't understand).

6. Saving Can Bring Temptations

We can be tempted to save for wrong reasons—out of fear and greed or a desire for independence from God and others.

If you save out of fear, then you are not trusting God (1 Tim. 6:17). If you do it out of greed, you've missed the whole point (Prov. 1:19; Mark 8:36; Luke 12:15). And once you've acquired some wealth, you don't want to become like the miser we read about in Ecclesiastes 5:13 or the "rich fool" we read about in Luke 12. The problem with both isn't that they saved; it's that they were focused only on themselves and put their faith in riches rather than God.

We can be tempted to save for wrong reasons—out of fear and greed or a desire for independence from God and others.

Hoarders are consumed by the need to preserve wealth rather than risk it for productive uses and the good of others. It also brings curses (Prov. 11:26) and judgment (Luke 12:16–21; James 5:3; Ps. 39:6; Eccl. 5:13; Zech. 9:3).

7. Balance Is Key

Finding the right balance is the key.

On the one hand, we need to set aside something and invest it wisely for future needs. On the other, we want to be generous and remain dependent on God, recognizing that he is the source of our provision and alone controls the future.

Whatever we decide, it must be out of a heart of gratitude to God for his kind generosity toward us—a God who is gracious, loving, and merciful (Ps. 107:8–9)—and based on the biblical wisdom he has given us on this topic.

The Christian Ethics of Saving

According to James Derksen (1993), for many people in this world, the goal of life is to gain enough material goods to make one's present life comfortable and to save up at least enough to make one's future secure. The Christian should recognize, however, that these goals are not consistent with the teaching of scripture. But what is the Biblical view of money and possessions? With so many needy persons in the world, should Christians save for the future or give all their money away? Are there other responsibilities which Christians must consider in their use of money? In answering these questions, we will first present the Biblical view of money and possessions. Next, we will lay out the teaching of scripture on how Christians are to use their financial and material resources. Finally, we will discuss the Christian view on saving in the light of the Biblical teaching.

Before beginning our investigation, it is useful to define money and saving. Money is the right of an individual to control a portion of the resources of the world. For the purposes of this paper, the terms money, wealth, possessions and property will be used interchangeably and include stocks, bank accounts, material goods, land, and any other means of storing value. Saving, then, is the storing up of money for future use.

The Biblical View of Material Goods, Riches, and Money

In the beginning when God created the world, He created it ``very good" (Gn 1:10,12,18,21,25,31; cf Mk. 7:18-19; Rom. 14:14-18; 1 Tim. 4:4). Thus, in their original form, all the material things of this world were good. Because God created the world, He is the absolute owner of everything (Ex. 9:29; 19:5; Job 41:11; Ps. 24:1-2; 50:12; I Co. 10:26). As a result, He has the right to do whatever He wants with His world.

Although God is the owner of everything, He has entrusted the resources of the world to men both to supply their needs and for them to care for it (Gn. 1:29-30; 2:15-17). Jesus taught this principle in the Parable of the Talents (Mt. 25:14-30; Lk. 19:12-27). This parable teaches that we are God's stewards on earth to whom He has entrusted various resources, abilities, and opportunities. We are expected to use them to benefit His kingdom. If we hide the things, He has entrusted to us by either refusing to use them or misusing them, we will be punished (Mt. 8:10-12). If we use them well, we honour God and demonstrate that we are able to handle greater responsibilities.

Also, within the framework of God's ultimate ownership, the scriptures teach that private property and wealth is not intrinsically evil. The Law protected private property (Ex. 22:1-15; Dt. 27:17; Pr. 22:28). The Ten Commandments, for example, assumed private property by prohibiting the stealing or coveting a neighbour's land, house, or animals (Ex. 20:15,17; Dt. 5:19,21). Often the Old Testament speaks of wealth as God's blessing for the righteous (Ps. 25:12-13; 128:1-2; Pr. 3:9-10; 10:22; 11:24-28; 22:9; cf Dt. 7:12- 13; 28:1-14). Abraham and Job were examples of righteous men of whom God approved and who had vast personal wealth (Gn. 12:2; 14:4; Job 1:3; 42:10). Jesus also permitted private property by using the house of His disciple, Simon Peter (Mk. 1:29) and by commanding His followers to give and lend to the poor (which assumes they had material possessions to give -- Mt. 5:42; 6:2-4; Lk. 6:34-35).

Although the scriptures teach that it is not wrong to have material possessions, they also give a very clear warning of the dangers of wealth. The primary danger of wealth is that it often gives one a false sense of security in the material goods of this world. This sense of security leads one to forget the true God and run after the god of wealth (Hos. 13:6; cf Dt. 8:10-20; 32:15; Pr. 30:7-9; Lk. 12:13-21). Jesus warned that the deceitfulness of wealth is like weeds which choke out the life of a small plant (Mt. 13:1- 23; Mk. 4:1-20; Lk. 8:4-15). This deceitful temptation of wealth can be seen in the life of a rich young man who came to Jesus, wanting to follow Him. When Jesus showed the young man that he would have to give up his riches to truly follow Him, the young man could not part from the deceptive god of his riches (Mt. 19:16-30; Mk. 10:17-31; Lk. 18:18-29). After the rich young man had left Jesus, Jesus said, ``I tell you the truth, it is hard for a rich man to enter the kingdom of heaven. Again, I tell you, it is easier for a camel to go through the eye of a needle than for a rich man to enter the kingdom of God" (Mt. 19:23-24; cf Mk. 10:24-25; Lk. 18:24-25). Wealth not only temps us to forget God, but it also ``is the root of all kinds of evil" (I Tim. 6:5, 9-11). Greed is perhaps the most common result of wealth, a form a idolatry which will keep one out of the kingdom of heaven (Ro. 1:29; I Co. 6:9-10; Eph. 5:5; Col. 3:5). Wealth can also lead on into pride (Jer. 9:23; Ez. 28:4-5; cf Hos. 12:8), murder (I Ki. 21:1-16; Jam. 5:1-5), perversion of justice (Ex. 23:8; Dt. 16:19; 27:25; cf I Sam. 8:3), false teaching for dishonest gain (II Pe. 2:3,14), and disregard for the poor (Ez. 16:49-50; Am. 6:1,4-7; Jam. 5:1-5; cf Is. 5:8-10; Lk. 16:19-31). [3] Although the benefits of wealth are attractive, there are also many dangers associated with it which have very serious consequences.

Instead of looking to the false security of wealth, Christians are called to seek first after the kingdom of God and allow Him to provide for them (Mt. 6:19-33; Lk. 12:22-31; I Ti. 2:7). They are to ask their Heavenly Father for their daily needs (Mt. 6:11, 7:7-11; Lk. 11:3,11-13; Jam. 1:17). If they trust God in this way, He will not only supply their needs, but also give them spiritual riches (Eph. 1:18; 2:7; cf Rev. 2:9).

Biblical Teaching on How to Use Money

According to the scriptures, there are five major categories for which Christians should use the money God has entrusted to them. First, the Christian is commanded to pay taxes. This is also why you pay taxes, for the authorities are God's servants, who give their full time to governing. Give everyone what you owe him: if you owe him taxes, pay taxes; if revenue, then revenue;

if respect, then respect; if honour, then honour" (Rom. 13:6-7; cf Mt. 22:15-22; 17:24-27; Mk. 12:13-17; Lk. 20:20-26; Tit. 3:1).

Second, Christians are to pay their employees, those who work for them, a fair wage (Jer. 22:13; Mal 3:5; Jam. 5:1-6; cf Job 31:38-39; Mt. 20:1-15; Col. 4:1). In ancient times, workers often worked on a daily basis, earning just enough each day to provide for the needs of their family for one day. As a result, those who hired workers were prohibited from holding back wages overnight, which would effectively make the workers family go hungry (Lv. 19:3; Dt. 24:14-15). Thus, workers should not only be paid fairly but also in a timely manner.

Thirdly, Christians are responsible to provide for their families. If anyone does not provide for his relatives, and especially for his immediate family, he has denied the faith and is worse than an unbeliever" (I Tim. 5:8; cf Ex. 20:12; Dt. 5:16; Mt. 15:3-9; Mk. 7:9-15; II Cor. 12:14; Eph. 6:2-3; I Tim. 5:4,16). The family here includes at least parents, brothers, sisters, grandparents, as well as oneself.

Fourthly, Christians should support God's work on this earth. According to the Old Testament Law, the people of Israel were commanded to set apart a tithe of all they grew or raised. A part of the tithe was to provide for the needs of the priests and Levites (Lev. 27:30-32; Num. 18:21-32). The other years, the Israelites were to east their tithe before the Lord, but were commanded not to neglect the Levites (Dt. 14:22-29; 26:12-13). In the New Testament, Christians are commanded to financially support church elders and those who preach the good news. Do not you know that those who work in the temple get their food from the temple, and those who serve at the altar share in what is offered on the altar? In the same way, the Lord has commanded that those who preach the gospel should receive their living from the gospel" (I Cor. 9:13-14; cf Mt. 10:10; Lk. 10:7; I Co. 9:7-14; I Tim. 5:17-18; Tit. 3:13). An example of this type of giving was the support Paul received from the Macedonians and the Philippians (II Co. 11:7- 12; Philip. 2:25; 4:14-20).

Fifthly, Christians are commanded to help the poor and needy. The Old Testament Law protected the people of Israel from getting deep into poverty. One way this was effected was through laws which kept the rich from exploiting the poor. Every fifty years there was a year of Jubilee during which land that had been sold was returned to the family who had originally owned it, and Israelite slaves were set free (Lv. 25:8-55). Every seven years there was a Sabbath year during which all debts between Israelites were to be cancelled (Dt. 15:1-5; 31:10; Neh.

10:31). The Law also commanded that an Israelite was to lend and give generously to the poor even though the year for cancelling debts was near and he would lose his money (Deut. 15:7-11). In addition, the land was to lie fallow and the poor allowed to eat its produce (Ex 23:10-11). These laws kept the poor from getting hopelessly in debt and keep the rich from taking advantage of the poor.

Other Old Testament laws helped the poor more directly. Every three years the tithe was to be given to widows, orphans, aliens, and the Levites (Dt. 14:28-29; 26:12-13). In addition, the Law prohibited the Israelites from going back to pick up what was left over after they harvested their fields. Whatever was left was to be left for the aliens, fatherless, and widows to glean for themselves (Lv. 19:10; Dt. 24:19-22; Rut 2).

The New Testament teaches Christians to give to many types of people. They should give to those who have needs. ``Religion that God our Father accepts as pure and faultless is this: to look after orphans and widows in their distress ..." (Jam. 1:27; cf Mt. 6:2-4; Lk. 14:12-14; 19:1-9; Acts. 6:1-7; Gal. 2:10). Jesus taught that in the end times those who did not give to the needy would be condemned to eternal punishment. The reason He will give the condemned ones in the final judgment will be, I tell you the truth, whatever you did not do for one of the least of these (hungry, thirsty, strangers, in need of clothes, sick, and in prison), you did not do for me (see Mt. 25:31-46; cf Lk. 16:19-31). Thus, our treatment of the poor indicates our true attitude towards Christ and His kingdom. Christians are particularly commanded to take care of the needs of their Christian brothers and sisters. This is how we know what love is: Jesus Christ layed down his life for us. And we ought to lay down our lives for our brothers" (I Jn. 3:16; cf Ro. 12:13; I Ti. 5:3,5; Phlm. 1:18-19). This type of giving obviously includes more than just financial support.

Not only are Christians to give to those who merit their help, but also to anyone who asks their help (Mt. 5:42; Lk. 6:30) and even their enemies (Lk. 6:27-36; Ro. 12:20). Jesus demonstrated this type of giving through the parable of the good Samaritan who helped a strange, wounded Jew on a road where danger lurked, even though Jews and Samaritans were bitter enemies (Lk. 10:25-37).

In contrast to the Biblical teaching on giving, there are circumstances under which a Christian should not give. A Christian is to keep away from and even refuse to eat with another Christian who is idle (II Thes. 3:6-12, 14-15; cf I Thes. 5:14; Tit. 3:14). ``If a man will not work, he shall not eat" (II Thes. 3:10). The motivation for not giving to such a person is to help bring the person back into a lifestyle which pleases God (II Thes. 3:14-15). The church is also not to give to widows who have families in the church who can provide for them (I Tim. 5:4), widows who are not living exemplary lives (I Tim. 5:9-10), and widows who would be exposed to temptation through the giving (I Tim. 5:11-15). There are two basic motivations behind for these reasons not to give. One, in the case of not giving to widows with families in the church, is to keep the church from being burdened with responsibilities that rightly belong to the family. The other cases are motivated by a love and desire to either help a person leave a lifestyle of sin or help prevent a person from entering such a lifestyle. Thus, the only Biblical reasons for not giving are to fulfill other responsibilities and to lovingly help another person live in a right relationship with God.

The Bible says much about how a Christian must give. The basic reason to give is love. ``If I give all I possess to the poor ..., but have not love, I gain nothing" (I Cor. 13:3). Christians should also give with generosity (II Co. 9:8-11; Mt. 20:1-16), cheerfully what they have decided in their hearts to give (II Co. 9:7), and through hospitality (Ro. 12:13; I Pe. 4:9; III Juan 5-8). James emphasizes the need to make one's faith active: ``Suppose a brother or sister is without clothes adn daily food. If one of you says to him, ÔGo, I wish you well; keep warm and well fed,' but does nothing about his physical needs, what good it is?" (Jam. 2:14-17).

Scripture also gives Christians reasons why they should give. They should give because they are content with what God has given them (I Tim. 6:6-8), and because they have been changed from their previous way of life: ``He who has been stealing must steal no longer, but must work, doing something useful with his own hands, that he may have something to share with those in need" (Eph. 4:28). This command to work in order to give implies planning ahead so one can give more. The Christian should also give with a goal of having equality (II Cor. 8:1-5) and so that men would praise God (II Cor. 9:12-14).

There are numerous exemplary examples of giving in the New Testament. A widow in the temple gave all she had (Mk. 12:41-44; Lk. 21:1-4). In the early church the believers shared everything they had, and ``from time to time those who owned lands or houses sold them, and brought the money from the sales ..., and it was distributed to anyone as he had need" (Acts 4:32-35; cf Acts 2:44).[4] This sharing among believers in Jerusalem was extended to sharing among the church as a whole when Paul began collecting money from the Gentile churches to provide for the needs of the impoverished church in Jerusalem (Ro. 15:25-27; I Co. 16:1-4; II Co. 8:1-9:5).[5] The church in Macedonia was especially exemplary in its giving. Paul says of them:

``Out of the most severe trial, their overflowing joy and their extreme poverty welled up in rich generosity. For I testify that they gave as much as they were able, and even beyond their ability. Entirely on their own, they urgently pleaded with us for the privilege of sharing in this service to the saints. And they did so not as we expected, but they gave themselves first to the Lord and then to us in keeping with God's will." (II Co. 8:1-15)

Paul's example of giving certainly merits our attention. His goal as an apostle was to spread the gospel free of charge (I Cor. 9:15-18; cf II Cor. 2:7; 11:7-12), even though he deserved to be supported by the gospel (I Cor. 9:13-14). He chose rather to be supported by established churches (II Cor. 11:8-9; Phlp. 2:25; 4:14-20), to be an example by working hard to support himself (II Thes. 3:7-9), or even going hungry and homeless at times (I Cor. 4:11; II Cor. 6:5,10; 11:27). His was content in all situations and chose to share both his life and the gospel (Phlp. 4:10-13; I Thes. 2:8-9). Finally, he was willing to spend everything he had his very life for those with whom he worked (II Cor. 12:13-15).

The ultimate example for the Christian is that of Jesus, who gave up all His power and prestige in heaven so that he could come to earth, suffer and die for those who hated Him. ``For you know the grace of our Lord Jesus Christ, who though he was rich, yet for your sakes became poor, so that you through his poverty might become rich" (II Co. 8:9; cf I John 3:16).

Biblical Ethics of Saving Money

The Christian ethics of saving are derived primarily from the Biblical teaching on the use of money. The most important principle we must remember is that God owns everything, and we are but stewards of what He has entrusted to us. Thus, we must honour God by saving in a manner consistent with the principles of money use presented in scripture.

The teaching of scripture on the dangers of wealth reminds us that our savings must never become our security (Mt. 19:16-30; Mr. 10:17-31; Lk. 12:13-21; 18:18-29). We must not store up earthly goods at the expense of heavenly ones because we cannot possibly serve God and money at the same time (Mt. 6:19, 24; Lk. 16:13-15). If fact, wealth and the desire to have more will tend to draw us away from God (Mt. 13:1-23; Mk. 4:1-20; Lk. 8:4-15). Therefore, must constantly be on guard against the deceitfulness of wealth, to make sure the deceitfulness of our hearts has not led us astray (Jer. 17:9). But how do we know where our hearts are? One way to distinguish is to ask ourselves the question, ``Is our money at all hindering us from following God?"[6] The deceitfulness of wealth not only comes from having large amounts of money. What about that small amount of money tucked away in the bank in case of emergency? Does it make us feel more comfortable and secure? Or could we give it away without feeling just a little bit anxious? Honestly answering these questions will help us test the true treasure of our hearts.

The question then arises, should we save at all then or just depend on God's daily providence? The scriptures are clear that we can (and should) save, at leave for a short time, to responsibly fulfil our financial obligations to the government, those who work for us, and our families (Prov. 6:6-8; 30:25). For example, except in special cases, it would be irresponsible for us to give away all our money at church if we knew that our family would go hungry that evening as a result. We should also save money whenever it would help us be better stewards of God's money. An example of this type of saving would be saving up to buy some big item instead of buying it on credit and paying interest.

When we look at the vast horrors of poverty in this world, it seems ridiculous that we would even think of saving up for ourselves instead of helping those in need. It is beyond the scope of this paper to consider all the ramifications of poverty for the Christian. However, we must remember that God commands us to give to the needy and warns us against neglecting our duty to help them (Mt. 6:2-4; 25:31-46; Lk. 14:12-14; 16:19-31; Jam. 1:27; Gal. 2:10). In considering how much to give and how much to save, we must remember to distinguish between what we really need to fulfil our responsibilities and what we would like. God promises to provide for our needs but does not promise to give us our selfish desires (Mt. 6:33; Jam. 4:3; cf I Tim. 6:8). Finally, in considering how much to give to the poor, we should follow the example of Jesus, ``who though he was rich, yet for your sakes became poor, so that you through his poverty might become rich" (II Co. 8:9; cf I Juan 3:16).

Therefore, we can see that saving is neither intrinsically good or evil. Nevertheless, saving is a tool which we can use to be more effective stewards of the resources God has entrusted to us. Therefore, both the quantity and use of our savings must be consistent with the teaching of scripture about the use of money.

The key principles that are fundamental to understand and underline in our minds:

God owns it all.

Few Christians would argue with this. But if we really *believe* it, there are three revolutionary implications that follow. First, God has the right to whatever He wants whenever He wants it. As His steward, I have no rights – only responsibilities. Second, every spending decision is a spiritual decision – there is nothing more spiritual about giving to a ministry than there is about buying a car or paying off a debt. Third, the way I use my money is an indicator of my spiritual health. My chequebook reveals everything that needs to be said about my goals, priorities, convictions, relationships, and even the way I use my time.

We are in a growth process.

Our time on earth is temporary and is to be used for our Lord. Money and material possessions are an important part of this picture. Our eternal position and reward are closely intertwined with the way we handle the property God has entrusted to us. When we are *faithful* in keeping this charge, we move closer to Christ. If we fail in this responsibility, our growth is hindered. It's as simple as that.

The amount is not important.

Remember – God owns it all. Therefore, hold with an open hand whatever He chooses to give you, whether it be little or much.

Faith requires action.

Simply knowing that God owns it all is not enough. The lazy and wicked servant in Jesus' story (Matthew 25:26-27) knew that he had been entrusted with his master's money, but he did nothing with it. God's resources should be used with an eye to God's goals and objectives.

What does a good steward look like? We'd suggest that there are five key indicators of the faithfulness with which he's carrying out his responsibilities. First, he gives generously in proportion with the level of his resources and abilities (2 Corinthians 8:12). Second, he exercises self-control by maintaining a debt-free lifestyle (Romans 13:8; Galatians 5:23. Third, he pays his taxes with integrity and an attitude of thanksgiving (Matthew 22:21; Romans 13:7). Fourth, he sets financial goals with an eye to the needs of his family and loved ones (1 Timothy 5:8). And fifth, he seeks the counsel of wise advisors and remains accountable to others in all his financial dealings (Proverbs 15:22).

If you need help applying these concepts to the day-to-day realities of your financial situation, don't hesitate to give our counsellors a call. They'd be happy to listen to your concerns and assist you with some practical suggestions. They can also provide you with referrals to advisors and counsellors who specialize in helping families with financial issues.

The wisdom of ants in focus

Wisdom is not sold and so no one can buy it. The wisdom of ants in focus: It is one precious thing unique to humans but when a man becomes too lazy to reason up in life, he becomes less sensitive and reasonable to the ants.

These creatures are very small but with the huge wisdom, they can awe you to the max. King Solomon, the richest and the wisest man ever to live placed emphasis on the wisdom of ants and tells us to go to the ants and learn her ways.

"Go to the ants; You sluggard, observe its ways and be wise (Proverbs 6:6). Solomon identified the ants as astonishing creatures by trying to understand their ways and wisdom.

Today many of us are chasing celebrities and big men in our societies and countries to learn their ways but the bible said to go to the ants. In this article, I would like to share with you how the ants use their wisdom to organize themselves and prepare for the future.

I and you should also go to the ants and learn their ways for there is nothing precious than acquiring wisdom free of charge from the ants. You can go to the woods, your backyard, kitchen, garden or anywhere you think you can find ants, observe them, know how they organize themselves, march, transports items and how they build Ant cities. You can spend months to fully understand their ways.

What Does The Bible Say About The Wisdom Of Ants?

The bible said, "The ants are a people not strong, yet they prepare their meat in the summer" (Proverbs 30:25).

When you observe very well, you will see that the ants march in two different directions (inwards and outwards) and as they move together in lines to carry pieces of food items, some could be food crumbs left by people or little bones of fish and other items.

They gather all this food in their storage house during summer. And when winter or rainy season comes they will stay indoors and enjoy their labor.

The most amazing part is how they get to know its summer and so they should store up some food to face winter or rainy seasons. No one tells them, but with their wisdom, they are able to do that.

The wisdom of ants has intrigued many people like me and scientists. They are able to count the number of their eggs and ranges them in order of age. As the ants march to find food they leave tracks for their friends to trace to find the food source and back.

If you destroy their path or direction, quickly they will know that there is a breach so they will form another path by changing direction. Nobody directs them. The ants are also very sensitive to the aroma of their food and so they can figure out where food lies within a certain distance.

The ants are very disciplined although they have no central leader, they love themselves, they care for each other, and are ready to die for themselves. There is nothing like greediness among them. Together they work and together they enjoy the fruits of their works. The wisdom of ants is hard to comprehend by people. Though they have tiny bodies at least they can carry food items ten times heavier than their bodies.

Personally, I observed their movements since I was a kid. Tracing where they are moving from and to is very interesting and as they march and bypass each other they seem to exchange greetings. Together they can carry dead insects like cockroaches, ants, spiders and other dead flies into their storehouse.

Recently I found myself reading the book of Job in the Bible and to my dismay, I got to know that God deprived the peacock and the ostrich wisdom. What an amazing God? he gave the peacock beautiful wings and yet without wisdom, she doesn't mind stepping on her own babies killing them.

"She is hardened against her young once, as though they were not hers; her labour is in vain without fear; Because God hath deprived her of wisdom, neither had he imparted unto her understanding" (Job 39:16-17).

God who made all animals know them very well in terms of their abilities, reasons, understanding, and everything. As for the horse, he gave them the courage to run fiercely in battlegrounds without being scared of javelins, sword, arrows and other war weapons.

Lessons from the Wisdom of Ants

Now let us know about **Ants lessons** or **Ants bible lessons**. God himself is wisdom, I mean he is the source of wisdom, he is the one who gives to anyone who deserves it and deprives anyone or any creäture that doesn't deserve it. Every Christian believer must know that the fear of the Lord is the beginning of wisdom (Proverbs 28:28).

So, **if** you fear the Lord then automatically you are wise or full of wisdom. This in no small way means the ants fear the Lord and so they are one of the wisest creatures to live. Scientists have found out that they make use of the **moonlight** and the **sunlight** for navigation in their nest. So, movement would never be difficult for them.

1. Caring

The second Ants lesson or Ants bible lesson is how they care for each other (Philippians 2:4). We must learn from the ants, how they want each other successful by showing support to help anyone who is in need. If you wish your friend good, then surely good things shall come unto you as well.

2. Love

Again, the next ant's Bible lesson is about how they show love to the extent of laying down their lives for others. They are ever ready to die for each other and the bible tells us that there is no love greater than for one to lay down his life for his friends (John 15:13).

3. Investments

The next ant's lesson, I want everyone to take note of is how they invest in the future. They are wise enough to know that a time will come that would be difficult for them to get food or march searching for food, building ants cities and so forth so they prepare themselves by storing up food in their room. In the future when winter comes, or rainy seasons come, they wouldn't be in any trouble.

So, I and you have to know that it is good to invest our future lives into something profitable to help us feel secure in the future, we shouldn't wait for a catastrophe to hit us before we take a step.

We can invest in the future by acquiring, health insurance, life, insurance, car insurance and all the good insurances you can think of. We should also be futuristic by planning ahead of time.

Finally, lessons from the ants tell us that, we should share what we have with everyone who deserves the profits of our labour. Here it is for us to avoid cheating if we are to share something among ourselves. The ants share the food they have stored in their nest without discrimination.

More to Learn from the Ants

I like almost every movement of the ants with the exception that;

1. **They sting**: When they come into contact with your body, they feel threatened, so to defend themselves they have to sting. It's very painful and the pains could last for a couple of minutes or hours.

2. **They can invade your house for food**:

Just like I said earlier, they are very sensitive so if you leave food crumbs in your room they can show up as uninvited guests marching around your room. They like food items like sugar, bread, roasted groundnut, dead insects, etc.

In conclusion, as human beings, we are God's greatest creation, we worth more than everything God created because he made us in his own image.

And for God to tell us to go to the ants to learn wisdom, it sounds a little satirical, because the kind of wisdom God gave us to take care of all creatures surpasses that of the ants. But why then should we go to the ants? God said that because some of us are too lazy to the extent that we feel bossy or lazy to sweat and earn from our sweats.

A lazy man shouldn't eat, but today, in our world lazy people are eating and enjoying more than those who are working and they do this through illegal means by indulging in fraud, bribery and corruption, lies and many more.

These so people lack wisdom and so they should go to the ants and learn wisdom. We have to love one another, care for one another, obey rules even if there are no rulers or leaders in our societies, workplaces, and countries.

The wisdom of human beings should put things in order for the benefits of everyone. Thanks for reading, don't forget to drop your comments below. Share this article with friends. Let them know about **the wisdom of ants** and how we should learn from them.

Figure 2: The abundance of money in south african Rands (R) in the house of the Lord.

What Does the Bible Say About Money and Wealth?

Frequently Asked Questions

- Will God make me prosperous and wealthy?
- Why do people have money problems, even when they are serving God?
- Why hasn't God answered my prayers to get out of debt?
- Where does it say God will prosper me?

This article summarizes what the Bible says about money, wealth, riches and poverty.

The Bible Does not Promise Wealth

There is no promise in the Bible that being a Christian will lead to a good job, wealth, freedom from debt, etc.

One verse is sometimes cited:

For I know the plans I have for you," declares the Lord, "plans to prosper you and not to harm you, plans to give you hope and a future. 1 (TNIV, Jeremiah 29:11)

In context, this verse was directed specifically to the Israelite exiles in Babylon. The original Hebrew word translated as "prosperity" can mean peace, completeness, safety, health, satisfaction or blessings[1]. It does not imply financial prosperity. This translation probably comes closer to the intended meaning:

For I know the plans I have for you," says the Lord. "They are plans for good and not for disaster, to give you a future and a hope. (NLT, Jeremiah 29:11)

God's faithful people may be rich or poor (2 Chronicles 17:3-5, Job 1:1-3, Matthew 27:57, Mark 12:41-44, Luke 16:19-22, 19:2-9, Proverbs 22:2, Luke 6:20).

Wealth Is not a Sign of God's Favour

In Jesus' time it was a common belief that great wealth was a sign of God's favour and poverty was God's punishment for sin.

Some Old Testament verses do reflect the idea that poverty is a natural consequence of foolish actions (Proverbs 6:9-11, 20:13, 23:21).

However, Jesus denied that wealth is a sign of God's favour or that poverty is God's punishment for sin. This is shown most clearly in His *Parable of the Rich Man and Lazarus* (Luke 16:19-31). At least part of the reason the rich man ended up in hell was because of his hard-heartedness toward the beggar Lazarus. His great wealth was obviously not a sign of God's favour. The beggar Lazarus ended up in heaven although he was about as impoverished as a man could be. His poverty was obviously not a sign of sinfulness or foolishness.

Despite the Bible's many warnings against it, the idea that wealth is a sign of God's favour and that the poor have done something to deserve their condition persists as an undercurrent today that is sometimes used to justify a callous attitude toward those who are poor.

Related verses: Proverbs 15:16-17, Ecclesiastes 5:10-12, Luke 1:52-53, 6:20, 6:24-25.

Wealth Is a Gift from God to Be Used in His Service

Jesus saw wealth as a gift from God to be used in His service (Matthew 25:14-30). Those who have been blessed with wealth must share generously with the poor (Matthew 25:31-46), and avoid the sins of arrogance (1 Timothy 6:17-19), dishonesty (Exodus 20:15, Mark 10:19, Luke 3:12-14) and greed (Luke 12:13-21).

Those of us who are blessed with wealth beyond our need have a responsibility to share generously with the less fortunate. We should view our wealth as a gift from God, entrusted to us, to carry out His work on earth.

If anyone has material possessions and sees his brother in need but has no pity on him, how can the love of God be in him? (NIV, 1 John 3:17)

Command those who are rich in this present world not to be arrogant nor to put their hope in wealth, which is so uncertain, but to put their hope in God, who richly provides us with everything for our enjoyment. Command them to do good, to be rich in good deeds, and to be generous and willing to share. In this way they will lay up treasure for themselves as a firm foundation for the coming age, so that they may take hold of the life that is truly life. (NIV, 1 Timothy 6:17-19)

Wealth Is Dangerous

Then Jesus looked around and said to his disciples, "How hard it will be for those who have wealth to enter the kingdom of God!" And the disciples were perplexed at these words. But Jesus said to them again, "Children, how hard it is to enter the kingdom of God! It is easier for a camel to go through the eye of a needle than for someone who is rich to enter the kingdom of God." They were greatly astounded and said to one another, "Then who can be saved?" Jesus looked at them and said, "For mortals it is impossible, but not for God; for God all things are possible." (NRSV, Mark 10:23-27)

It is not that wealth is intrinsically evil, or that poverty is blessed. Rather, a devotion to gathering wealth is incompatible with devotion to God. God must always be the most important thing in our lives:

"No one can serve two masters. For you will hate one and love the other, or be devoted to one and despise the other. You cannot serve both God and money." (NLT, Luke 16:13)

The craving for wealth and possessions can lead us into all kinds of temptation. While we spend evenings and weekends earning extra money, we are depriving our families of our love and attention. We may take unfair advantage of our customers, employers, or employees. We may attempt to rationalize our greed by closing our minds- and hearts to the needs and rights of others. In the process, we could end up being stingy, bitter and isolated.

Do not wear yourself out to get rich; have the wisdom to show restraint. Cast but a glance at riches, and they are gone, for they will surely sprout wings and fly off to the sky like an eagle. (NIV, Proverbs 23:4-5)

What good will it be for a man if he gains the whole world, yet forfeits his soul? Or what can a man give in exchange for his soul? (NIV, Matthew 16:26)

Those who want to get rich fall into temptation and a trap and into many foolish and harmful desires that plunge people into ruin and destruction. For the ***love*** of money is a root of all kinds of evil. Some people, eager for money, have wandered from the faith and pierced themselves with many griefs. (TNIV, 1 Timothy 6:9-11, emphasis added)

"Do not store up for yourselves treasures on earth, where moth and rust destroy, and where thieves break in and steal. But store up for yourselves treasures in heaven, where moth and rust do not destroy, and where thieves do not break in and steal. For where your treasure is, there your heart will be also. (NIV, Matthew 6:19-21)

Related verses: Matthew 13:22, Luke 12:15, 1 Timothy 6:17-19, James 5:1-5.

Avoid Dishonesty

The rationalization required to obtain and keep dishonest gain can make a person cold, cynical and separated from God. It may be taking unfair advantage or misrepresenting the facts to employers, employees, customers, clients or associates. It may be stealing, fraud, inflating insurance claims, cheating on taxes, "pirating" music and movies, wilful non-payment of debts, or any form of dishonesty for personal gain. In whatever form, dishonest gain brings only fear of discovery - never peace of mind.

'You shall not oppress your neighbour, nor rob him. The wages of a hired man are not to remain with you all night until morning. (NAS, Leviticus 19:13)

The LORD abhors dishonest scales, but accurate weights are his delight. (NIV, Proverbs 11:1)

He who walks righteously and speaks what is right, who rejects gain from extortion and keeps his hand from accepting bribes, who stops his ears against plots of murder and shuts his eyes against contemplating evil-- this is the man who will dwell on the heights, whose refuge will be the mountain fortress. His bread will be supplied, and water will not fail him. (NIV, Isaiah 33:15-16)

Let every person be subject to the governing authorities; for there is no authority except from God, and those authorities that exist have been instituted by God... For the same reason you also pay taxes, for the authorities are God's servants, busy with this very thing. Pay to all what is due them - taxes to whom taxes are due, revenue to whom revenue is due, respect to whom respect is due, honour to whom honour is due. (NRSV, Romans 13:1, 6-7)

Related verses: Exodus 20:15, Leviticus 19:35-36, Proverbs 21:6, Amos 8:4-8, Micah 6:10-13, Mark 10:19, Luke 3:12-14.

9 Biblical Principles of Money & Possessions

Money, money, money.

You think about money.

You work for money.

You save money.

You spend money.

You tithe your money (sometimes **using online giving**).

You stress over money.

Even though money isn't an essential thing in your life. A significant portion of your life will revolve around earning, saving, giving, and spending money. So your relationship with money isn't something you can just brush aside as unspiritual or unnecessary.

To help you manage your money well, we reviewed over a hundred Bible verses about money, money management, and money trouble to see what God has to say about this critical piece of life.

In this post, we're going to address these three big topics relate bible verses about money:

1. What is money?
2. How many bible verses about money are there?
3. What does the Bible say about money?
4. Why does the church talk so much about money?

Now, when it comes to breaking down what the Bible has to say about money, we identified...

Nine principles about money you need to know:

- God owns everything
- Money is a tool
- Worship with your money
- Get that money
- Fight for contentment
- Kill greed in your heart
- Be mindful of debt
- Manage your finances
- Mo' money, mo' problems

This post is a doozy as there are a lot of bible verses about money. It will take you 10 minutes or more to read.

Let's get ready to dig in!

What is money?

In short, money is a medium of exchange. It's an agreed upon item you can use to make a purchase, trade, or pay off a debt. The medium of exchange will differ in many countries. What is more, the use of money makes it a whole lot easier to get what you need instead of having swap your pet dog for a box of cereal.

Here's something you need to know about money: Bible verses or not, money is amoral.

Money doesn't have a life. It cannot act on its own. It cannot do good deeds, and it cannot commit crimes. Basically, it's neither good or bad. No matter how many bible verses about money there is.

Money can only do what you tell it to do.

Money is *not* the root of all evil. But the love of money *is* the root of all evil (1 Tim. 6:10).

If the concept of money is so simple and it doesn't have a power emanating from its core drawing us to it, then why do we sweat over money so much? Why does the church talk so often about money? These are great questions, which leads me to my next point.

How many bible verses about money are there?

The bible is packed with over 2,000 scriptures about money, tithing in the Bible, and possessions. That's twice as many bible verses about money than faith and prayer combined.

What does the bible say about money?

The bible says many things about money, but the heart of the matter is this: money can become something that rules our lives—an idol of sorts. God's desire is for us to have life to the full and He knows that worshiping money will keep us from that.

From the seduction of success to the lure of lust, many things in this world will vie for your affection and devotion. But the most significant idol you will face is money (Matt. 6:24).

Why does the Church talk so much about money?

There are two good reasons why the Church talks so often about money. First, the reason the Church talks about money is because God talks about money. Consider these statistics on bible verses about money:

- 16 out of 38 of Jesus' parables deal with money and possessions
- Nearly 25% of Jesus' words in the New Testament deal with biblical stewardship
- 1 out of 10 verses in the Gospels deal with money
- There are more than 2,000 scriptures on tithing in the Bible, money, and possessions in the Bible, which is twice as many as faith and prayer combined

Many verses in the Bible talk about money, and for a good reason too, which leads me to my next point.

Second, bible verses about money are frequently used because there's a direct correlation between the way we handle our money and our faith.

When it comes to money, we will either *worship wealth* or worship *with* our wealth.

Read that again.

There's a big difference between the two.

From the seduction of success to the lure of lust, many things in this world will vie for your affection and devotion. But the most significant idol you will face is money (Matt. 6:24).

God desires our devotion, and he knows you will come face-to-face with the temptation of money, which is why he speaks so often about it.

Money itself may be amoral. But it's our attachment to and our worship of money that will lead us into sin and making poor financial decisions.

9 things Bible verses say about money

In the words of Jesus, “For where your treasure is, there your heart will be also” (Luke 12:34). After reviewing **Bible verses about money**, there are nine big principles that come to the surface, including:

1. God owns everything
2. Money is about discipleship
3. Worship with your money
4. Get that money
5. Fight for contentment
6. Kill greed in your heart
7. Be mindful of debt
8. Manage your finances
9. More money, more problems

What the Bible has to say about money isn’t limited to these nine principles.

Remember, there are roughly 2,000 Bible verses about money and possessions, which means there are way more nuances talked about in the Bible than these nine.

All I’m saying is that these nine principles appear to be the most prominent. Because, you know, *"the love of money is the... "*

1. God owns everything

God doesn’t talk about money because he’s broke and needs a helping hand. Far from it. God owns everything (Ex. 19:5). Since God is the rightful owner of everything we have, this means the money we earn actually belongs to God. Practically speaking, God calls us to manage the money we accumulate on his behalf not to have a love of money. This is the essence of biblical stewardship.

- **Exodus 19:5:** Now therefore, if you will indeed obey my voice and keep my covenant, you shall be my treasured possession among all peoples, for all the earth is mine.
- **Job 41:11:** Who has first given to me, that I should repay him? Whatever is under the whole heaven is mine.

- **Psalm 24:1:** The earth is the LORD's and the fullness thereof, the world and those who dwell therein,
- **1 Timothy 4:3-5:** Who forbid marriage and require abstinence from foods that God created to be received with thanksgiving by those who believe and know the truth. For everything created by God is good, and nothing is to be rejected if it is received with thanksgiving, for it is made holy by the word of God and prayer.

2. Money is about discipleship

Money is a tool God uses to help us live and love like Jesus. Regardless of how much—or how little—money you have, God is at work in your life through your circumstances. He is leading you to a deeper trust in him. This is exactly what we see in Philippians 4:11-12:

"Not that I am speaking of being in need, for I have learned in whatever situation I am to be content. I know how to be brought low, and I know how to abound. In any and every circumstance, I have learned the secret of facing plenty and hunger, abundance and need."

Are you struggling financially? Or are you swimming in a financial abundance? Do you have a love of money that isn't healthy?

Regardless of your situation, instead of asking "why" or just saying "thanks," be sure to ask God what you can learn since there is a connection between your faith and money.

- **Matthew 6:24:** "No one can serve two masters, for either he will hate the one and love the other, or he will be devoted to the one and despise the other. You cannot serve God and money."
- **Luke 12:34:** "For where your treasure is, there will your heart be also."
- **Luke 16:11-12:** "If then you have not been faithful in the unrighteous wealth, who will entrust to you the true riches? And if you have not been faithful in that which is another's, who will give you that which is your own?"

3. Worship with your money

If you're not careful, it can be easy to place your hope in money. Money is something we can hold in our hands or look at in our bank account. We feel the weight of its absence or possess a sense of self-sufficiency when we have it in abundance. In Bible verses about putting your hope in money, you're going to come across a ton of warnings:

- "Be careful!"
- "Guard your heart!"
- "Don't be a fool with your money!"

When it comes to money, wealthy people are not the only ones who will be tempted to sin. Regardless of how much money you have, you'll be tempted to sin in different ways.

Instead of placing your hope in money or whatever generates income, place your hope in God. He owns everything, and he will provide you with what you need to live your life for him.

Check out these Bible verses about putting your hope in money:

1 Samuel 2:7: "The LORD makes poor and makes rich; he brings low and he exalts."

4. Fight for contentment

It's difficult to be content—with yourself, with your work, with your family, and with your possessions. We are bombarded with a slew of messages and images everywhere we go that entice us to pursue something "better." From wanting a new car, getting a bigger house, or coveting a promotion at work, the world we live in compels us to be dissatisfied with who we are and what we have.

Discontentment may not sound like a big deal on the surface. But it's a subtle sin leading us to desire more or something different, yet it leaves us lacking and empty-handed in the end.

Living in a state of discontentment can tempt you to take on unnecessary debt, cheat on your spouse, or make unwise decisions at work in an attempt to get ahead.

Now, contentment is more than just being happy with who you are and what you have—contentment is rooted in God's love for you. It's learning to be satisfied wholly in Christ regardless if you have a little or a lot of money.

In Bible verses about contentment, we learn two essential truths:

1. You have to fight for contentment
2. You can be content

In your fight for contentment, God will empower you to obtain this mysterious and elusive virtue. It's not something beyond your reach. In the words of the Apostle Paul, "I can do all thing through him who strengthens me" (Phil. 4:13).

Here is a list of Bible verses about contentment to help you fight for contentment:

- **Job 36:11:** "If they listen and serve him, they complete their days in prosperity, and their years in pleasantness."
- **Proverbs 19:23:** "The fear of the LORD leads to life, and whoever has it rests satisfied; he will not be visited by harm."
- **Psalm 37:16-17:** "Better is the little that the righteous has than the abundance of many wicked. For the arms of the wicked shall be broken, but the LORD upholds the righteous."
- **2 Corinthians 12:9-10:** "But he said to me, 'My grace is sufficient for you, for my power is made perfect in weakness.' Therefore I will boast all the more gladly of my weaknesses, so that the power of Christ may rest upon me. For the sake of Christ, then, I am content with weaknesses, insults, hardships, persecutions, and calamities. For when I am weak, then I am strong."
- **Philippians 4:11-13:** "Not that I am speaking of being in need, for I have learned in whatever situation I am to be content. I know how to be brought low, and I know how to abound. In any and every circumstance, I have learned the secret of facing plenty and hunger, abundance and need. I can do all things through him who strengthens me."
- **Philippians 4:19:** "And my God will supply every need of yours according to his riches in glory in Christ Jesus."

- **1 Timothy 6:6-12:** "But godliness with contentment is great gain, or we brought nothing into the world, and we cannot take anything out of the world. But if we have food and clothing, with these we will be content. But those who desire to be rich fall into temptation, into a snare, into many senseless and harmful desires that plunge people into ruin and destruction. For the love of money is a root of all kinds of evils. It is through this craving that some have wandered away from the faith and pierced themselves with many pangs." But as for you, O man of God, flee these things. Pursue righteousness, godliness, faith, love, steadfastness, gentleness. Fight the good fight of the faith. Take hold of the eternal life to which you were called and about which you made the good confession in the presence of many witnesses."

5. Get that money

We've written at length on scriptures about work. In short, here's what you need to know: In general, you need to work to earn money. Some people are unable to work for different reasons. Whether it's an illness or physical handicap, you may be unable to obtain gainful employment.

To support people who are unable to provide for him or herself, in general, God has provided three different layers of support:

1. The family
2. The church
3. The state

Without getting into the details about the biblical view of wealth and poverty, we do find many examples and commands in the Bible verses about money about taking care of the poor, widows, and orphans. God has provided a safety net for people in three different ways: the family, the church, and the state.

Now, on the other side of this coin, we also observe many examples and commands in the Bible encouraging Christians to work diligently. Since we are created in the image of God, we are hardwired to work, to create. What is more, God has commanded us to work.

When it comes to God's command to work, it was given before sin entered the world and the human heart. Work is rooted in God's good created order.

There are many positive benefits associated with gainful employment. However, since sin has entered the world, we will be tempted to worship work (make it our god), reject work (become lazy), or twist work (do something sinful).

In Christ, God redeems work.

He took the “thorns and thistles” we work among (Gen. 1:18), and he wore a crown of thorns on his head as a reminder that he is the “Kind of kings and the Lord of lords” (Rev. 19:16).

Practically, this means through faith in Jesus, you will be empowered to glorify God in your work and for the good of others.

Check out these verses about providing for the poor, and working hard for your money:

- **Exodus 22:22:** "You shall not mistreat any widow or fatherless child.”
- **Exodus 22:25:** “If you lend money to any of my people with you who is poor, you shall not be like a moneylender to him, and you shall not exact interest from him."
- **Deuteronomy 22:22:** “If a man is found lying with the wife of another man, both of them shall die, the man who lay with the woman, and the woman. So you shall purge the evil from Israel.”
- **Deuteronomy 23:19:** “You shall not charge interest on loans to your brother, interest on money, interest on food, interest on anything that is lent for interest.”
- **Deuteronomy 24:20:** "When you beat your olive trees, you shall not go over them again. It shall be for the sojourner, the fatherless, and the widow.”
- **Proverbs 10:22:** "The blessing of the LORD makes rich, and he adds no sorrow with it.”
- **Proverbs 11:14:** "Where there is no guidance, a people falls, but in an abundance of counselors there is safety.”
- **Proverbs 13:11:** "Wealth gained hastily will dwindle, but whoever gathers little by little will increase it.”
- **Proverbs 17:16:** "Why should a fool have money in his hand to buy wisdom when he has no sense?”
- **Proverbs 22:1:** "A good name is to be chosen rather than great riches, and favor is better than silver or gold.”
- **Psalm 49:10-12:** "For he sees that even the wise die; the fool and the stupid alike must perish and leave their wealth to others. Their graves are their homes forever, their dwelling places to all generations, though they called lands by their own names. Man in his pomp will not remain; he is like the beasts that perish.”

- **Malachi 3:5:** "Then I will draw near to you for judgment. I will be a swift witness against the sorcerers, against the adulterers, against those who swear falsely, against those who oppress the hired worker in his wages, the widow and the fatherless, against those who thrust aside the sojourner, and do not fear me, says the LORD of hosts."
- **Matthew 19:21-26:** "Jesus said to him, 'If you would be perfect, go, sell what you possess and give to the poor, and you will have treasure in heaven; and come, follow me.' When the young man heard this he went away sorrowful, for he had great possessions. And Jesus said to his disciples, 'Truly, I say to you, only with difficulty will a rich person enter the kingdom of heaven. Again I tell you, it is easier for a camel to go through the eye of a needle than for a rich person to enter the kingdom of God.' When the disciples heard this, they were greatly astonished, saying, 'Who then can be saved?' But Jesus looked at them and said, 'With man this is impossible, but with God all things are possible.'"
- **Matthew 21:12-13:** "And Jesus entered the temple and drove out all who sold and bought in the temple, and he overturned the tables of the money-changers and the seats of those who sold pigeons. He said to them, 'It is written, 'My house shall be called a house of prayer,' but you make it a den of robbers.'"
- **Luke 3:14:** "Soldiers also asked him, 'And we, what shall we do?' And he said to them, 'Do not extort money from anyone by threats or by false accusation, and be content with your wages.'"
- **Luke 12:33:** "Sell your possessions, and give to the needy. Provide yourselves with moneybags that do not grow old, with a treasure in the heavens that does not fail, where no thief approaches and no moth destroys."
- **Acts 4:34:** "There was not a needy person among them, for as many as were owners of lands or houses sold them and brought the proceeds of what was sold."
- **Acts 6:1:** "Now in these days when the disciples were increasing in number, a complaint by the Hellenists arose against the Hebrews because their widows were being neglected in the daily distribution."
- **Acts 8:20:** "But Peter said to him, 'May your silver perish with you, because you thought you could obtain the gift of God with money!'"

- **Acts 20:35:** "In all things I have shown you that by working hard in this way we must help the weak and remember the words of the Lord Jesus, how he himself said, 'It is more blessed to give than to receive.'"
- **Galatians 6:5:** "For each will have to bear his own load."
- **1 Timothy 5:3-10:** "Honour widows who are truly widows. But if a widow has children or grandchildren, let them first learn to show godliness to their own household and to make some return to their parents, for this is pleasing in the sight of God. She who is truly a widow, left all alone, has set her hope on God and continues in supplications and prayers night and day, but she who is self-indulgent is dead even while she lives. Command these things as well, so that they may be without reproach. But if anyone does not provide for his relatives, and especially for members of his household, he has denied the faith and is worse than an unbeliever. Let a widow be enrolled if she is not less than sixty years of age, having been the wife of one husband, and having a reputation for good works: if she has brought up children, has shown hospitality, has washed the feet of the saints, has cared for the afflicted, and has devoted herself to every good work." For the love of money is a root of all kinds of evils. It is through this craving that some have wandered away from the faith and pierced themselves with many pangs."
- **1 Timothy 6:17-19:** "As for the rich in this present age, charge them not to be haughty, nor to set their hopes on the uncertainty of riches, but on God, who richly provides us with everything to enjoy. They are to do good, to be rich in good works, to be generous and ready to share, thus storing up treasure for themselves as a good foundation for the future, so that they may take hold of that which is truly life."
- **2 Thessalonians 3:6-14:** "Now we command you, brothers, in the name of our Lord Jesus Christ, that you keep away from any brother who is walking in idleness and not in accord with the tradition that you received from us. For you yourselves know how you ought to imitate us, because we were not idle when we were with you, nor did we eat anyone's bread without paying for it, but with toil and labour we worked night and day, that we might not be a burden to any of you. It was not because we do not have that right, but to give you in ourselves an example to imitate. For even when we were with you, we would give you this command: If anyone is not willing to work, let him not eat. For we hear that some among you walk in idleness, not busy at work, but busybodies. Now such persons we command and encourage in the Lord Jesus Christ to

do their work quietly and to earn their own living. As for you, brothers, do not grow weary in doing good. If anyone does not obey what we say in this letter, take note of that person, and have nothing to do with him, that he may be ashamed."

- **James 1:27:** "Religion that is pure and undefiled before God the Father is this: to visit orphans and widows in their affliction, and to keep oneself unstained from the world."
- **1 John 2:15-17:** "Do not love the world or the things in the world. If anyone loves the world, the love of the Father is not in him. For all that is in the world—the desires of the flesh and the desires of the eyes and pride of life—is not from the Father but is from the world. And the world is passing away along with its desires, but whoever does the will of God abides forever."
- **Revelation 3:17:** "For you say, I am rich, I have prospered, and I need nothing, not realizing that you are wretched, pitiable, poor, blind, and naked."

6. Kill greed in your heart

Who is a greedy person? Is it a politician? How about the CEO of a multi-billion-dollar company? Or are athletes, musicians, or actors or actresses greedy? Regardless of what image comes to your mind, here's something you need to know about greed: It's not good, and you'll have to fight it off in your life.

Greed is bad, and it's something all of us will have to fight in our life. In the words of the Apostle Paul, "Put to death, therefore, whatever belongs to your earthly nature: sexual immorality, impurity, lust, evil desires and greed, which is idolatry" (Col. 3:5).

There's a good chance you probably don't think you have a greed problem. But let me ask you these questions:

- Are you satisfied with how much money you make?
- Do you want to purchase more things?
- Does your desire for more money and possessions choke out your interest in God?

In life, the presence of greed will come and go in waves, which is why it's a good idea to keep your finger on the pulse of your heart and to kill the presence of sin in your life with the antidote of the gospel.

- **Genesis 12:1-3:** Now the LORD said to Abram, 'Go from your country and your kindred and your father's house to the land that I will show you. And I will make of you a great nation, and I will bless you and make your name great, so that you will be a blessing. I will bless those who bless you, and him who dishonours you I will curse, and in you all the families of the earth shall be blessed.'"
- **Deuteronomy 8:18:** "You shall remember the LORD your God, for it is he who gives you power to get wealth, that he may confirm his covenant that he swore to your fathers, as it is this day."
- **Proverbs 15:27:** "Whoever is greedy for unjust gain troubles his own household, but he who hates bribes will live."
- **Proverbs 28:22:** "A stingy man hastens after wealth and does not know that poverty will come upon him."
- **Proverbs 28:25:** "A greedy man stirs up strife, but the one who trusts in the LORD will be enriched."
- **Matthew 13:22:** "As for what was sown among thorns, this is the one who hears the word, but the cares of the world and the deceitfulness of riches choke the word, and it proves unfruitful."
- **Mark 7:21-22:** "For from within, out of the heart of man, come evil thoughts, sexual immorality, theft, murder, adultery, coveting, wickedness, deceit, sensuality, envy, slander, pride, foolishness."
- **Luke 12:13-21:** "Someone in the crowd said to him, 'Teacher, tell my brother to divide the inheritance with me.'But he said to him, 'Man, who made me a judge or arbitrator over you?' And he said to them, 'Take care, and be on your guard against all covetousness, for one's life does not consist in the abundance of his possessions.' And he told them a parable, saying, "The land of a rich man produced plentifully, and he thought to himself, 'What shall I do, for I have nowhere to store my crops?' And he said, 'I will do this: I will tear down my barns and build larger ones, and there I will store all my grain and my goods. And I will say to my soul, "Soul, you have ample goods laid up for many years; relax, eat, drink, be merry."' But God said to him, 'Fool! This night your soul is required of you, and the things you have prepared, whose will they be?' So is the one who lays up treasure for himself and is not rich toward God."

- **Romans 7:7:** "What then shall we say? That the law is sin? By no means! Yet if it had not been for the law, I would not have known sin. For I would not have known what it is to covet if the law had not said, 'You shall not covet.'"
- **1 Corinthians 5:11:** "But now I am writing to you not to associate with anyone who bears the name of brother if he is guilty of sexual immorality or greed, or is an idolater, reviler, drunkard, or swindler—not even to eat with such a one."
- **1 Corinthians 6:9-10:** "Or do you not know that the unrighteous will not inherit the kingdom of God? Do not be deceived: neither the sexually immoral, nor idolaters, nor adulterers, nor men who practice homosexuality, nor thieves, nor the greedy, nor drunkards, nor revilers, nor swindlers will inherit the kingdom of God."
- **Ephesians 5:5:** "For you may be sure of this, that everyone who is sexually immoral or impure, or who is covetous (that is, an idolater), has no inheritance in the kingdom of Christ and God."
- **1 Thessalonians 2:5:** "For we never came with words of flattery, as you know, nor with a pretext for greed—God is witness."
- **Hebrews 13:5:** "Keep your life free from love of money, and be content with what you have, for he has said, "I will never leave you nor forsake you."
- **1 Peter 5:2-3:** "Shepherd the flock of God that is among you, exercising oversight, not under compulsion, but willingly, as God would have you; not for shameful gain, but eagerly; not domineering over those in your charge, but being examples to the flock."
- **2 Peter 2:14-15:** "They have eyes full of adultery, insatiable for sin. They entice unsteady souls. They have hearts trained in greed. Accursed children! Forsaking the right way, they have gone astray. They have followed the way of Balaam, the son of Beor, who loved gain from wrongdoing."
- **James 5:1-6:** "Come now, you rich, weep and howl for the miseries that are coming upon you. Your riches have rotted and your garments are moth-eaten. Your gold and silver have corroded, and their corrosion will be evidence against you and will eat your flesh like fire. You have laid up treasure in the last days. Behold, the wages of the laborers who mowed your fields, which you kept back by fraud, are crying out against you, and the cries of the harvesters have reached the ears of the Lord of hosts. You have lived on the earth in luxury and in self-indulgence. You have fattened your hearts in a day of slaughter. You have condemned and murdered the righteous person. He does not resist you."

7. Be mindful of debt

There's a good chance you have financial debt. How can I make such a bold statement? Simple. According to research, total household debt in the United States was $13.15 trillion at the end of 2017. So, there's a good chance you have some debt.

Since debt is so common in the United States, and is a leading cause of financial stress, it's essential to get God's perspective on debt so that you can best manage your finances.

So what does the Bible say about debt?

After you review the Bible verses about debt, you'll discover three principles:

1. God *does not* forbid debt
2. God *does* highly caution against debt
3. Taking on debt is generally a bad thing

Even though God doesn't forbid debt, you still want to be cautious when you consider taking on debt. It's also a good idea to seek the advice of a financial advisor or godly counsel to speak into your financial situation.

If you are in debt (not including your mortgage), prayerfully consider the steps you can take to get out of debt as soon as possible—especially when it comes to paying off credit cards.

- **Deuteronomy 28:12:** "The LORD will open to you his good treasury, the heavens, to give the rain to your land in its season and to bless all the work of your hands. And you shall lend to many nations, but you shall not borrow."
- **Ecclesiastes 5:4:** "When you vow a vow to God, do not delay paying it, for he has no pleasure in fools. Pay what you vow."
- **Proverbs 6:1-5:** "My son, if you have put up security for your neighbour, have given your pledge for a stranger, if you are snared in the words of your mouth, caught in the words of your mouth, then do this, my son, and save yourself, for you have come into the hand of your neighbour: go, hasten, and plead urgently with your neighbour. Give your eyes no sleep and your eyelids no slumber; save yourself like a gazelle from the hand of the hunter, like a bird from the hand of the fowler."

- **Proverbs 20:16:** "Take a man's garment when he has put up security for a stranger, and hold it in pledge when he puts up security for foreigners."
- **Proverbs 22:7:** "The rich rules over the poor, and the borrower is the slave of the lender."
- **Proverbs 22:26:** "Be not one of those who give pledges, who put up security for debts."
- **Psalm 37:21:** "The wicked borrows but does not pay back, but the righteous is generous and gives."
- **Matthew 5:42:** "Give to the one who begs from you, and do not refuse the one who would borrow from you."
- **Matthew 6:24:** "No one can serve two masters, for either he will hate the one and love the other, or he will be devoted to the one and despise the other. You cannot serve God and money."
- **Luke 6:35:** "But love your enemies, and do good, and lend, expecting nothing in return, and your reward will be great, and you will be sons of the Most High, for he is kind to the ungrateful and the evil."
- **Luke 14:28:** "For which of you, desiring to build a tower, does not first sit down and count the cost, whether he has enough to complete it?"
- **Romans 13:7-8:** "Pay to all what is owed to them: taxes to whom taxes are owed, revenue to whom revenue is owed, respect to whom respect is owed, honour to whom honour is owed. Owe no one anything, except to love each other, for the one who loves another has fulfilled the law."

8. Manage your money

Wouldn't it be nice if there was a single Bible verse about money management that would deliver you from all of your financial worries? I wish there was something I can share, but this isn't the case—at all. To manage your money, there are two steps you need to take:

1. Make a plan
2. Work your plan

First, you need a plan.

In your financial plan, you need to answer the following questions:

- What's your total income?
- How much do you need to tithe?
- How much money do you need to save and invest?
- What are your monthly expenses and debt repayments?

After you know your income and expenses, here are four more questions you should consider:

- What costs can you reduce?
- How much more money can you pay toward your debts?
- Can you give more money to your church or a non-profit organization?
- How can you save more money?

These steps will help you make a plan, and there are many personal budget templates you can find online to guide your efforts.

Second, after you make a plan, you have to work your plan.

For this step, you have to look in the mirror and realize there's nobody else in your life who can take responsibility for your financial situation.

You have to pay your bills.

You have to use mobile giving or online giving to your church.

You have to fight the temptation of accumulating more debt.

Thankfully, you're not left alone in your decisions. You can find forgiveness for poor financial choices in Christ, and you can be hopeful that he will help you to get out of your financial troubles.

- **Deuteronomy 15:7:** "If among you, one of your brothers should become poor, in any of your towns within your land that the LORD your God is giving you, you shall not harden your heart or shut your hand against your poor brother."

- **Ecclesiastes 7:12:** "For the protection of wisdom is like the protection of money, and the advantage of knowledge is that wisdom preserves the life of him who has it."
- **Proverbs 3:9-10:** "Honour the LORD with your wealth and with the first fruits of all your produce; then your barns will be filled with plenty, and your vats will be bursting with wine."
- **Proverbs 10:4:** "A slack hand causes poverty, but the hand of the diligent makes rich."
- **Proverbs 14:8:** "The wisdom of the prudent is to discern his way, but the folly of fools is deceiving."

  Luke 14:28-30: "For which of you, desiring to build a tower, does not first sit down and count the cost, whether he has enough to complete it? Otherwise, when he has laid a foundation and is not able to finish, all who see it begin to mock him, saying, 'This man began to build and was not able to finish.'"

9. More money and more problems

We are prone to worry about money, which makes perfect sense. From the increase in cost of living, taking on too much debt, to unexpected expenses, there are a ton of reasons why we may feel anxious about our financial situation. Naturally, to resolve our situation, the first thing many of us do—including myself—is to think about making more money.

If I could only get a raise.

It would be awesome if I scored that sweet promotion.

I'd love to score big on the lottery someday.

Wouldn't it be nice to have a high-paying side hustle?

These are some thoughts that may go through your mind from time-to-time (though I'm not advocating for gambling). But here's the deal about making more money:

Acquiring more money may not fix your financial problems.

According to Richard Watts, author of *Fables of Fortune*, more money may actually cause you more problems.

Making more money sounds good on the surface, and it may be the best course of action you can take. But it's not the silver bullet to every financial problem.

To solve your financial problems, Bible verses about money worries encourage us to take this first step:

Trust the Lord.

I know this sounds trite, but hear me out.

Yes, you'll need to make a plan, curve your spending, and get out of debt. But the heart of your problem isn't your finances.

The heart of your problem is whether or not you're worshipping your money or worshiping with your money.

Here's what we learn about God and our money from the Bible verses about money trouble:

- God will provide for you
- God is aware of your financial situation
- God will forgive you if you've made sinful financial choices
- God doesn't want you to worry about money
- God wants you to know that life is more about your relationship with God
- God wants you to seek him first before you go after more money

Today, if you're feeling stressed about your financial situation, take a moment to read these **Bible verses about money** worries, meditate on them, and take a break to pray.

Bible Verses About Money

- **1 Chronicles 29:14:** "But who am I, and what is my people, that we should be able thus to offer willingly? For all things come from you, and of your own have we given you."
- **Ecclesiastes 5:10:** "He who loves money will not be satisfied with money, nor he who loves wealth with his income; this also is vanity."

- **Proverbs 3:9-10:** "Honour the LORD with your wealth and with the first fruits of all your produce; then your barns will be filled with plenty, and your vats will be bursting with wine."
- **Proverbs 11:28:** "Whoever trusts in his riches will fall, but the righteous will flourish like a green leaf."
- **Proverbs 12:25:** "Anxiety in a man's heart weighs him down, but a good word makes him glad."
- **Proverbs 23:4-5:** "Do not toil to acquire wealth; be discerning enough to desist. When your eyes light on it, it is gone, for suddenly it sprouts wings, flying like an eagle toward heaven."
- **Psalm 55:22:** "Cast your burden on the LORD, and he will sustain you; he will never permit the righteous to be moved."
- **Psalm 56:3:** "When I am afraid, I put my trust in you."
- **Psalm 62:10:** "Put no trust in extortion; set no vain hopes on robbery; if riches increase, set not your heart on them."
- **Psalm 94:19:** "When the cares of my heart are many, your consolations cheer my soul."
- **Matthew 6:19-21:** "Do not lay up for yourselves treasures on earth, where moth and rust destroy and where thieves break in and steal, but lay up for yourselves treasures in heaven, where neither moth nor rust destroys and where thieves do not break in and steal. For where your treasure is, there your heart will be also."
- **Matthew 6:25-34:** "Therefore I tell you, do not be anxious about your life, what you will eat or what you will drink, nor about your body, what you will put on. Is not life more than food, and the body more than clothing? Look at the birds of the air: they neither sow nor reap nor gather into barns, and yet your heavenly Father feeds them. Are you not of more value than they? And which of you by being anxious can add a single hour to his span of life? And why are you anxious about clothing? Consider the lilies of the field, how they grow: they neither toil nor spin, yet I tell you, even Solomon in all his glory was not arrayed like one of these. But if God so clothes the grass of the field, which today is alive and tomorrow is thrown into the oven, will he not much more clothe you, O you of little faith? Therefore, do not be anxious, saying, 'What shall we eat?' or 'What shall we drink?' or 'What shall we wear?' For the Gentiles seek after all these things, and your heavenly Father knows that you need them all. But seek first the kingdom of God and his righteousness, and all these things will be added to you.

Therefore, do not be anxious about tomorrow, for tomorrow will be anxious for itself. Sufficient for the day is its own trouble."

- **Matthew 11:28-30:** "Come to me, all who labour and are heavy laden, and I will give you rest. Take my yoke upon you, and learn from me, for I am gentle and lowly in heart, and you will find rest for your souls. For my yoke is easy, and my burden is light."
- **Mark 4:19:** "But the cares of the world and the deceitfulness of riches and the desires for other things enter in and choke the word, and it proves unfruitful."
- **Mark 8:36:**" For what does it profit a man to gain the whole world and forfeit his soul?"
- **Luke 8:14:** "And as for what fell among the thorns, they are those who hear, but as they go on their way they are choked by the cares and riches and pleasures of life, and their fruit does not mature."
- **Luke 12:22-34:** "And he said to his disciples, 'Therefore I tell you, do not be anxious about your life, what you will eat, nor about your body, what you will put on. For life is more than food, and the body more than clothing. Consider the ravens: they neither sow nor reap, they have neither storehouse nor barn, and yet God feeds them. Of how much more value are you than the birds! And which of you by being anxious can add a single hour to his span of life? If then you are not able to do as small a thing as that, why are you anxious about the rest? Consider the lilies, how they grow: they neither toil nor spin, yet I tell you, even Solomon in all his glory was not arrayed like one of these. But if God so clothes the grass, which is alive in the field today, and tomorrow is thrown into the oven, how much more will he clothe you, O you of little faith! And do not seek what you are to eat and what you are to drink, nor be worried. For all the nations of the world seek after these things, and your Father knows that you need them. Instead, seek his kingdom, and these things will be added to you. Fear not, little flock, for it is your Father's good pleasure to give you the kingdom. Sell your possessions, and give to the needy. Provide yourselves with moneybags that do not grow old, with a treasure in the heavens that does not fail, where no thief approaches and no moth destroy. For where your treasure is, there will your heart be also."
- **Luke 16:10-12:** "One who is faithful in a very little is also faithful in much, and one who is dishonest in a very little is also dishonest in much. If then you have not been faithful in the unrighteous wealth, who will entrust to you the true riches? And if you have not been faithful in that which is another's, who will give you that which is your own?"

- **John 14:27:** "Peace I leave with you; my peace I give to you. Not as the world gives do I give to you. Let not your hearts be troubled, neither let them be afraid."
- **Philippians 4:6:** "Do not be anxious about anything, but in everything by prayer and supplication with thanksgiving let your requests be made known to God."
- **Hebrews 13:5-6:** "Keep your life free from love of money, and be content with what you have, for he has said, 'I will never leave you nor forsake you.' So, we can confidently say, 'The Lord is my helper; I will not fear; what can man do to me?"
- **1 Peter 5:7:** "Casting all your anxieties on him, because he cares for you."

Figure 3: Notes in Rands showing the abundance of the good Lord in the house of the Lord.

More scriptures detailing the aspects of wealth and money, it must be said however that there are more than these:

Bible Verses About Wealth

God has told us that he will meet all of our needs. He will meet our needs, but we need to be careful of allowing money and wealth to become our master and our central focus, either by having too much, or too little.

We need to be good stewards of what He's given us, and to use what he has given us for His glory.

1 Philippians 4:19 And my God will meet all your needs according to his glorious riches in Christ Jesus.

Matthew 6:26 Look at the birds of the air; they do not sow or reap or store away in barns, and yet your heavenly Father feeds them. Are you not much more valuable than they?

Proverbs 23:5 Cast but a glance at riches, and they are gone, for they will surely sprout wings and fly off to the sky like an eagle.

Luke 16:13 No servant can serve two masters, for either he will hate the one and love the other, or he will be devoted to the one and despise the other. You cannot serve God and money.

1 Timothy 6:10 For the love of money is a root of all kinds of evil. Some people, eager for money, have wandered from the faith and pierced themselves with many griefs.

Proverbs 22:7 The rich rule over the poor, and the borrower is servant to the lender.

Luke 16:10-12 Whoever can be trusted with very little can also be trusted with much, and whoever is dishonest with very little will also be dishonest with much. So if you have not been trustworthy in handling worldly wealth, *who will trust you with true riches*? And if you have not been trustworthy with someone else's property, who will give you property of your own?

Proverbs 28:20 A faithful man will abound with blessings, but whoever hastens to be rich will not go unpunished.

Deuteronomy 8:18 But remember the LORD your God, for it is he who gives you the ability to produce wealth, and so confirms his covenant, which he swore to your ancestors, as it is today.

Proverbs 28:19 Whoever works his land will have plenty of bread, but he who follows worthless pursuits will have plenty of poverty.

Matthew 6:33 But seek first the kingdom of God and his righteousness, and all these things will be added to you.

Matthew 6:19-21 Do not lay up for yourselves treasures on earth, where moth and rust destroy and where thieves break in and steal, but lay up for yourselves treasures in heaven, where neither moth nor rust destroys and where thieves do not break in and steal. For where your treasure is, there your heart will be also.

Bible verses about true wealth in Christ

While we're not told that being wealthy is wrong necessarily, but we are warned against allowing our money and things become idols in our lives.

Instead of allowing money to become the central focus of our lives, we need to look to Christ to fulfill all our desires.

John 3:16 *For God so loved the world that he gave his one and only Son, that whoever believes in him shall not perish but have eternal life.*

Ephesians 1:17-21 I keep asking that the God of our Lord Jesus Christ, the glorious Father, may give you the Spirit of wisdom and revelation, so that you may know him better. I pray that the eyes of your heart may be enlightened in order that you may know the hope to which he has called you, ***the riches of his glorious inheritance*** in his holy people, and his incomparably great power for us who believe. That power is the same as the mighty strength he exerted when he raised Christ from the dead and seated him at his right hand in the heavenly realms, far above all rule and authority, power and dominion, and every name that is invoked, not only in the present age but also in the one to come.

Colossians 2:6-7 Therefore as you have received Christ Jesus the Lord, so walk in Him, having been firmly rooted and now being built up in Him and established in your faith, just as you were instructed, and overflowing with gratitude.

Romans 5:8 But God demonstrates His own love toward us, in that while we were yet sinners, Christ died for us. **Ephesians 2:8-9** For by grace you have been saved through faith; and that not of yourselves, it is the gift of God; not as a result of works, so that no one may boast.

Figure 4: Wealth in the form south African Notes displayed on the ground platforms

Quick generated wealth and pyramids schemes

The researchers and research have found that there are plenty of verses in the Bible that talk about how we should beware of get rich quick schemes, and how often, even if we are able to get rich quick that money tends to disappear faster than we could have imagined. Here's one of my favourite verses on the topic, in two translations:

- *Wealth from get-rich-quick schemes quickly disappears; wealth from hard work grows.* ***Proverbs 13:11***
- *Wealth gained hastily will dwindle, but whoever gathers little by little will increase it.* ***Proverbs 13:11***

The verse tells us that while get rich quick schemes can work sometimes, often because our heart isn't in the right place the money disappears as fast as it appeared. If instead, we work hard for the money and build it up over time, we'll appreciate it more, be more grateful and be more likely to put it to good use. Here's another verse talking about how sometimes, when we get too much money right away, it isn't as much of a blessing as we thought it would be.

An inheritance claimed too soon will not be blessed at the end. ***Proverbs 20:21***

Again, when we get money in a large lump sum, it can be more of a hindrance than a blessing. How many times have you heard of lottery winners having financial or family troubles years later?

A faithful man will abound with blessings, but whoever hastens to be rich will not go unpunished. ***Proverbs 28:20***

Who were the wealthiest men and women as per the historical account in the bible?

Although the Bible mentions a number of wealthy individuals, the richest person by far was King Solomon. His reign is described in the first half of the book of I Kings in the Old Testament. Interestingly enough, he did not ask for wealth. The story says that the Lord appeared to Solomon in a dream at night and asked what he should give him. Instead of requesting riches, honour, long life, or the defeat of his enemies in battle, Solomon requested an understanding heart, to be able to wisely judge his people. The request pleased God so much that he gave Solomon what he asked for, which was a wise and understanding — and also all the other things that he didn't ask for, as a bonus.

It takes the Bible several chapters to describe all of Solomon's wealth. He accumulated it in various ways. For instance, he sent out vessels for trading to Tyre, in what is now Lebanon, and the coast of Africa. These ships came back with gold, silver, ivory, and other valuable items. He heavily taxed his own subjects and also received tribute from the rulers of nearby lands. Additionally, visiting dignitaries brought him gifts. Notable among his visitors was the Queen of Sheba, who supposedly arrived with a great train of camels bearing gold, precious gems, spices, and other riches.

The Bible says that Solomon built two immense palaces, and within these palaces, all the cups and other vessels were made of gold, and none were made of silver. There was so much gold in Solomon's kingdom, in fact, that silver was considered as worthless as stones on the ground. Solomon also had an immense throne built of ivory overlaid with gold.

To give a rough idea of the Biblical estimation of a portion of Solomon's wealth, chapter 10 of I Kings says that Solomon received 666 talents of gold every year. According to Oxford Biblical Studies, a talent was about 75.5 pounds in our measurement. This means that Solomon's income included over 50,000 pounds of gold every year.

While it is nearly impossible to answer this question empirically, and with a great deal of certainty in terms of historicity, an educated guess is possible. It has been said that King Solomon (Book of 1 Kings) was one of the ten richest people in world history. According to the scripture, he collected over one billion dollars' worth of gold per year when calculated with the value of gold today. Solomon inherited a vast amount of wealth from his father, King David, who should be considered a close second as far as biblical wealth goes. Solomon was also known for his excessive taxation policies which would have added to his wealth. The King of Israel also collected tribute from countries and kingdoms that he controlled. Solomon also had a lucrative business partnership with Hiram, the King of Tyre in which he collected a large booty every three years. It would not be an overestimation to calculate Solomon's wealth to be over $10 billion dollars.

Financially speaking, the Bible covers a lot of ground. From the very poor (Ruth) to the very rich (Queen Esther) to people in between (Simon Peter) to people who shifted their financial status throughout their lives.

But who is the Bible's richest person? "Doesn't matter," you say. "The Bible isn't a contest of who is richest." And that's true, but we're not trying to win any contests here. This is speculation of a purely academic nature and, if we're fortunate, we might just pick up some financial wisdom along the way. Let's look at some contenders.

Abraham

Wealth was measured in a few ways in biblical times: cattle, land and actual currency like gold and silver. Abraham had all of that in huge numbers, and once even had to split some of his land with his nephew Lot because, as Genesis 13 puts it, "their possessions were so great that they were not able to stay together" (and as Biggie put it, "more money, more problems).

Isaac

Isaac inherited his father's wealth and it continued to expand, to the point where the Philistines once politely asked him to move because he'd gotten "too powerful" (Genesis 26:16). Isaac moved, but he couldn't seem to stop accumulating wealth. As God told him in Genesis 26:24, "I am the God of your father Abraham. Do not be afraid, for I am with you; I will bless you and will increase the number of your descendants for the sake of my servant Abraham."

Job

This one's a little complicated because Job is most famous for the relatively brief period of his life in which he had nothing except misery. But that instructive season was bookended by a time during which the Bible calls him "the greatest of all the men of the east." He held an early record for richest man in the hemisphere—a record he apparently later broke, when God gave Job back double the amount that he'd lost.

Solomon

Wisdom. Wealth. Solomon truly had it all, including a number of wives that might be charitably described as, uh, "plenty." 2 Chronicles 9:20 describes Solomon as being so rich that silver literally lost all value. In 1 Kings 10:10, the Queen of Sheba not exactly impoverished herself went on a sightseeing tour of Solomon's lands just to see if the rumours were true. His name is still associated with money today, and at least a few Crusades set out with the express purpose of finding and reclaiming his vast wealth.

Joseph

One of the Bible's most famous rags to riches stories, Joseph was a rich kid who was sold by his brothers into slavery. Then he ended up in jail and then, well, he became the second most powerful person in the ancient world's most powerful country, Egypt. Joseph had a head for economics and used his savvy to prepare Egypt for a drought God had warned Pharaoh about in a dream.

Many of these people lived centuries apart, making it a little difficult to adjust for what we'd today call "inflation." There are also a few mentions of some people we just don't have enough details on to make a judgment call (including the otherwise nameless "rich young ruler" in Mark 10). But we can make some educated guesses.

Scholars believe that Job was actually the oldest book in the Bible written even before Genesis, the "first" chronological book so it's safe to assume that Job was very wealthy relative to the comparatively few people alive at the time.

Second, while people like Abraham and Isaac were very wealthy, they were also very nomadic meaning there were some necessary limits on just how much wealth they could accumulate, since they were on the constantly on the move.

We know Joseph was very smart with money, but we also know he was second fiddle in Egypt. Second most powerful to an actual king is a pretty big deal, but it's not quite as big as being *the* king, and there's only one of those on our list. "Rich as Solomon" didn't become a saying for no reason at all, meaning he wins this round.

Unfortunately, he loses most other rounds. Despite being the richest man in the Bible, 1 Kings 11 describes how a bad relationship with his many, many wives led Solomon to stop worshipping God and he was punished by having his country torn apart after his death. It's a reminder that all the money in the world doesn't do you much good if you don't have a solid relationship to help you manage it.

Budgeting is still hard for couples, especially those who approach it from different backgrounds and beliefs. Is it a challenge? Sure, but it can be overcome. Bright peak Financial has put together a few ideas for how.

1. Abraham

Abraham is considered as the patriarch of the church and is known as the friend of God according to James 2:23. In Genesis 13:2, Abraham is described as rich in gold, silver, and cattle. During those times, having such material possessions is comparable to being an owner of a multi-billion business. As Abraham continued to profess his faith to the Lord, his possessions became even greater. In Genesis 24:1, it is said that God continued to bless him in many ways. Genesis 13:6 explains that Abraham continued to accumulate well to the point that he has to separate from his nephew Lot because their land could longer keep the two of them. What is even amazing is that everyone associated with Abraham were also gifted with material wealth.

2. Isaac

Isaac is Abraham's son and was also blessed with wealth. During the time of famine, Isaac continued to leave a prosperous life. In Genesis 26:12, Isaac was able to plant and harvest a hundred times more than other people. His wealth became the envy of the Philistines that it came to a point when he was forced to leave his land. Even in face of uncertainty, Genesis 26:17-32 says that Isaac continued to receive blessings no matter where he went.

3. Job

In the book of Job 1:1 in the Old Testament, Job was described to be a righteous man. Job 1:3 further describes him as the most illustrious man in the East because of his vast material possessions. In spite of his personal conflicts, Job showed his immense loyalty to God. In Job 42:10, he was given richness which surpassed what he previously owned because he remained steadfast in his belief even though he faced so many challenges in his life.

4. Solomon

If there is one Bible character that can be easily associated with richness and wealth, it is Solomon. Solomon is not only known as the wise king, but also as a man who lived with enormous material possession. In 2 Chronicles 9:20, it is said that he had so many gold in his possession to the point that silver lost its value. His wealth is so legendary that people up to this time are still looking for his hidden treasures. His wealth has become a staple of legends that various expeditions were launched to search for his treasures. It is said that part of the mission of the Crusaders to the Holy Land was to look for Solomon's treasures. There are even speculations that the lineage of the infamous Templar Knights have found the treasure and have hidden and protected them.

5. David

David is often associated with Goliath and their epic battle where the small child defeated the giant with a slingshot. But like Solomon, David lived a life of prosperity because of his faith in God. The amount of wealth he possessed was chronicled in the Book of Psalms. In Psalm 37:19, it is proclaimed that the righteous would still prosper in the midst of famine. And this was exactly what happened with David and his brethren. In 1 Chronicles 29:28, it is said that David enjoyed a life of prosperity, blessed with wealth and honour, and died after living a life full of contentment.

6. Joseph

Joseph (not the father of Jesus) was a wealthy man who became a victim of envy. He was a humble person in spite of his wealth. At the age of 30, he became second in command of the country of Egypt. According to Genesis 47:14, he was able to amass his wealth by selling grains. Joseph was blessed not only with business acumen, but with a strong economic outlook that he was able to look at the future and save his country.

Aside from wealth, these people of the Bible remained faithful to their God in spite of the trials and difficulties they encountered. They lived a life of prosperity and were continued to be blessed until their last breath. So, before you follow the adage "money is the root of all evil", think again.

King Solomon's Wealth

13 Every year King Solomon received over twenty-five tons of gold, 14 in addition to the taxes paid by the traders and merchants. The kings of Arabia and the governors of the Israelite districts also brought him silver and gold. 15 Solomon made two hundred large shields, each of

which was covered with about fifteen pounds of beaten gold, [16] and three hundred smaller shields, each covered with about eight pounds of beaten gold. He had them all placed in the Hall of the Forest of Lebanon.

[17] The king also had a large throne made. Part of it was covered with ivory and the rest of it was covered with pure gold. [18] Six steps led up to the throne, and there was a footstool attached to it, covered with gold. There were arms on each side of the throne, and the figure of a lion stood at each side. [19] Twelve figures of lions were on the steps, one at either end of each step. No throne like this had ever existed in any other kingdom.

[20] All of King Solomon's drinking cups were made of gold, and all the utensils in the Hall of the Forest of Lebanon were of pure gold. Silver was not considered valuable in Solomon's day. [21] He had a fleet of ocean-going ships sailing with King Hiram's fleet. Every three years his fleet would return, bringing gold, silver, ivory, apes, and monkeys.

[22] King Solomon was richer and wiser than any other king in the world. [23] They all consulted him, to hear the wisdom that God had given him. [24] Each of them brought Solomon gifts articles of silver and gold, robes, weapons, spices, horses, and mules. This continued year after year.

[25] King Solomon also had four thousand stalls for his chariots and horses, and had twelve thousand cavalry horses. Some of them he kept in Jerusalem and the rest he stationed in various other cities. [26] He was supreme ruler of all the kings in the territory from the Euphrates River to Philistia and the Egyptian border. [27] During his reign silver was as common in Jerusalem as stone, and cedar was as plentiful as ordinary sycamore in the foothills of Judah. [28] Solomon imported horses from Musri and from every other country.

Summary of Solomon's Reign

[29] The rest of the history of Solomon from beginning to end is recorded in *The History of Nathan the Prophet,* in *The Prophecy of Ahijah of Shiloh,* and in *The Visions of Iddo the Prophet,* which also deal with the reign of King Jeroboam of Israel.

Other accounts the richest person of all time

It is possible that it's **Augustus Caesar**, a Roman emperor who was estimated to have the biggest net worth ever ($4.6 trillion in modern money), but there are other contenders out there. Here's our list of the top 10 richest people of all time:

1. **Augustus Caesar** — Potentially the richest man of all time, he was the first emperor of the Roman Empire and valued at a rough estimate of $4.6 trillion in today's dollars. He personally owned a fifth of the wealth of an empire that accounted for about 30% of the gross domestic product of the whole world.
2. ***Possibly*: Emperor Shenzong of Song** — Also the leader of an empire that accounted for 30% of the world's GDP at the time and valued in the trillions, Emperor Shenzong of China is a contender for the richest man to ever live. It's possible he had the highest net worth ever. It's difficult, however, to separate his personal wealth from his country's, ranking him lower on our list.
3. ***Possibly*: King Solomon of Israel** — If you take the Bible as fact, the famous King Solomon's net worth would have been valued in the trillions, since every year, he demanded about 25 tons of gold from his subjects, eventually leading to his tragic downfall.
4. ***Possibly*: Genghis Khan** — Another of history's most profitable and terrifying emperors is Genghis Khan. Net worth estimates for him are all over the place, with some awarding him figures with the modern-day value of hundreds of trillions of dollars and others maintaining that Genghis Khan only had an extreme amount of land rather than great personal wealth. Either way, he's certainly a contender for the richest person to ever live.
5. **Jakob Fugger** — Despite being worth an estimated $400 to $500 billion, most people haven't learned about this Catholic, German, Renaissance-era mogul in their history lessons. He had a tight grip on the copper and textile industries in merchant-based Italy and even dealt out loans to the famous royals of the House of Habsburg. He started what many thinks of as the first European welfare housing program, the Fuggerei. (Only Catholics were allowed entry, though.)
6. **Mansa Musa** — According to his contemporaries, who simply could not fathom his wealth, this African king was the richest man in the world ever. How much is Mansa Musa worth today? With camel-loads of gold and salt, Mansa Musa's net worth has been valued by modern-day scholars to be around $400 to $415 billion in modern money.

7. **John D. Rockefeller** — Now, we've reached some modern rich people, starting with oil magnate John D. Rockefeller. Net worth figures for him are a bit skewed, but his $1.4 billion in olden-day money would be worth several hundred billion now. Some scholars estimate that he would be worth $400 billion today. For scale, that's three times more than today's richest person, Jeff Bezos.
8. **Andrew Carnegie** — Carnegie once said, "The man who dies rich dies disgraced." While he didn't exactly die a billionaire, giving away massive swaths of his wealth to more than 3,500 public libraries, the Carnegie net worth at his richest was valued in today's dollars between $300 and $372 billion.
9. **Nicholas II of Russia** — The revolutionaries considered their monarch to be the richest person in history. That being said, he spent wildly: His allotment of 24 million rubbles was usually spent by the end of the year.
10. **Osman Ali Khan** — The nizam of Hyderbad was named the wealthiest person ever by Time Magazine and used the world-famous Jacob Diamond as a paperweight.

Who Was the Richest Person in America's History?

The richest American ever is widely considered to be **John D. Rockefeller**, worth about $400 billion in inflation-adjusted dollars, or about 2% of the United States GDP. Members of his family continue to be some of the wealthiest people in U.S. history.

The richest women in the account of the bible

The Bible recorded a number of wise women often overlooked by Bible teachers. So, we continue to read some at random and let the Holy Spirit leads us to uncover gems as we press forward with the words of God. Today we read a very capable godly wealthy woman who was also a successful career woman on her own merit.

Her story was recorded in the book of Acts chapter 16:9-15. Apostle Paul was led by the Holy Spirit (in a night vision) to go to Macedonia to share the Good News of Jesus Christ. He and his co-worker (Luke) went at once. They reached Philippi, a major city there. On Sabbath they went to the riverbank prayer meeting and met Lydia and some women, instead of the devout men whom they had expected.

Lydia was converted immediately, baptized with her own household, and opened her house to Paul and the other disciples for meeting and stay. Her house became a gathering place (the first house church in Europe) for the believers. Indeed, the Holy Spirit had brought Paul to share the Good News to the right person at the right time and right place, and Lydia turned out to be the person in the vision of Paul!

What was outstanding about Lydia?

Background about her business: Lydia was "a dealer of purple cloth" from Thyatira. Tyrian purple is a vivid, purplish red. a highly prized crimson or purple dye of classical antiquity, costing equivalent USD$126278 / Troy Ounce. Each ounce required over 3500 molluscs to procure and so only the highly privileged could afford it. Indeed, ancient regimes often passed sumptuary laws to prohibit common folk from wearing.

Purple dye was a symbol of power and honour, and it was the most expensive and sought-after dye in the Roman world. She had to have plenty of capital to deal in purple dye and the making of purple garments for sale. She would be dealing her business with the royal and upper-class nobility exclusively. As the products were manufactured in Thyatira and in view of their high value, she would have to travel frequently personally to bring them to Philippi and her clients.

1. She was thus a rich, busy successful and influential business woman.
2. Yet she went for a prayer meeting at the riverbank on Sabbath. There was no Bible teacher or preacher but she and other women gathered and worshiped God as usual.

3. she was hungry and ready for the Good News. When she met Paul, she listened to his sharing and opened her heart to accept Jesus immediately.
4. She also ruled a household (which means she did not have a husband) who respected and obeyed her as their head.
5. She was able to bring her entire household to believe in Jesus and be baptized together with her.
6. Despite the fact that Christianity was not favoured by the influential religious Jews and the Roman authority, Lydia was brave, kind and generous and extended her hospitality to Paul immediately. By doing so, she had opened her home to Jesus, for the use of witnessing, sharing the Good News and worshiping God in spirit and in truth.
7. The Apostles and disciples of the early house churches met daily, and the head of the family was usually the pastor or deacon of the house church, so Lydia probably fitted into those important spiritual roles.

9. That night Paul had a vision: A man from Macedonia in northern Greece was standing there, pleading with him, "Come over to Macedonia and help us!" [10] So we decided to leave for Macedonia at once, having concluded that God was calling us to preach the Good News there. [11] We boarded a boat at Troas and sailed straight across to the island of Samothrace, and the next day we landed at Neapolis. [12] From there we reached Philippi, a major city of that district of Macedonia and a Roman colony. And we stayed there several days.

[13] On the Sabbath we went a little way outside the city to a riverbank, where we thought people would be meeting for prayer, and we sat down to speak with some women who had gathered there. [14] One of them was Lydia from Thyatira, a merchant of expensive purple cloth, who worshiped God. As she listened to us, the Lord opened her heart, and she accepted what Paul was saying. [15] She and her household were baptized, and she asked us to be her guests. "If you agree that I am a true believer in the Lord," she said, "come and stay at my home." And she urged us until we agreed.

[38] When the police reported this, the city officials were alarmed to learn that Paul and Silas were Roman citizens. [39] So they came to the jail and apologized to them. Then they brought them out and begged them to leave the city. [40] When Paul and Silas left the prison, they returned to the home of Lydia. There they met with the believers and encouraged them once more. Then they left town.

Mary of Nazareth

Mary's significant role in Scripture is widely known: Mary of Nazareth is the mother of Jesus. She gave birth to the saviour of the world when she was just a teenager.

The angel Gabriel told her of the unique role she would play in God's story and, while this certainly was frightening, Mary bravely embraced her calling and bore for all of humanity the saviour of the world. Six months after Elizabeth knew she was to become a mother; Gabriel was sent from God to Nazareth. Nazareth was a town in the country of Galilee. He went to a woman who had never had a man.

She was promised in marriage to a man named Joseph. Joseph was of the family of David. The angel came to her and said, 'You are honoured very much. You are a favoured woman. The Lord is with you. You are chosen from among many women.' When she saw the angel, she was troubled at his words. She thought about what had been said.

The angel said to her, 'Mary, do not be afraid. You have found favour with God. See! You are to become a mother and have a Son. You are to give Him the name Jesus. He will be great. He will be called the Son of the Highest. The Lord God will give Him the place where His early father David sat. He will be King over the family of Jacob forever and His nation will have no end.' (Luke 1:26-33)

2. Ruth the Moabite

Ruth the Moabite played a significant role in the coming of Jesus. After her husband died, she followed her mother-in-law Naomi to her homeland in Israel, where she met Boaz. They would become the great grandparents of King David, and eventually propagate the lineage of the messiah. Ruth faced great tribulation as a woman in an ancient context with no protection. But she boldly followed Naomi to the land of Israel, devoted herself to the Lord, and played a critical role in the victory of God over sin and death through her everyday faithfulness in the face of impossible circumstances.

The most popular Bible verse from the Book of Ruth:

"But Ruth replied, 'Don't urge me to leave you or to turn back from you. Where you go, I will go, and where you stay, I will stay. Your people will be my people and your God my

God (Ruth 1:16)".

3. Mary Magdalene

Mary Magdalene is often misunderstood. She was a faithful follower of Jesus. After Jesus healed her, she ventured alongside him in his ministry, meeting his needs and encouraging the disciples, eventually bearing witness to his crucifixion and burial.
Three days later, she would be the first witness of the empty tomb of Christ and one of the Core critical eye-witnesses to his resurrection that would later resource the gospel writers to give the church historical credibility.
"After the Sabbath, at dawn on the first day of the week, Mary Magdalene and the other Mary went to look at the tomb" (Matt. 28:1).

4. Rachel

Rachel waited earnestly, but patiently, to marry the love of her life: Jacob, who would later be named Israel. She was deceived by her father Laban and sister Leah who, after Jacob had worked seven years to acquire Rachel, was tricked into marrying Leah. So, Jacob worked another seven years and Rachel waited patiently another seven years in order to marry Jacob.

Though childless initially, she became the mother to Joseph, who by God's strength single-handedly saved all of Israel, and Benjamin, the last tribe in Israel to remain faithful to the Lord before the time of exile. Rachel's role in the history of redemption is difficult to underestimate, and she should be celebrated for her strength in the face of adversity by the strength of the Lord. "And God remembered Rachel, and God hearkened to her, and opened her womb." (Genesis 30:22)

5. Hannah

Hannah was initially childless, and prayed desperately for a son. She made a promise to God that if he permitted her to bear a son, she would devote him to God.

When God fulfilled this request, she faithfully kept her word. She left her son, Samuel, to be raised in the temple of the Lord while continuing to provide him guidance and mentorship along the way.

Hannah's faithfulness was never in question.
Samuel, her son, would go on to rescue Israel from centuries of slavery to the Canaanites and idolatry to Baal by anointing King David, whose heart was fully devoted to the Lord and who gifted God's people with most of the Psalms, which the church uses on a daily basis as a

source of strength, encouragement, and worship, both through seasons of blessing and tribulation. "It is not by strength that one prevails; those who oppose the Lord will be broken. The Most High will thunder from heaven; the Lord will judge the ends of the earth" (1 Sam. 2:10).

6. Eve

Eve is a very often misunderstood character in the Bible. While she and Adam both brought sin and death into the world through partaking of the tree of the knowledge of good and evil, she is the mother of the human race, and represents God's promise to beget the one who would crush the head of the devil and redeem humanity from sin once and for all. "The man called his wife's name Eve, because she was the mother of all living" (Gen. 3:20).

7. Deborah

The season of the judges was a tumultuous time for Israel. After Moses led Israel out of the land of Egypt and Joshua had led Israel into the land promised to Abraham to conquer the Canaanites, Israel fell into cycles of disobedience that prompted God's wrath to fall on Israel in the form of slavery to the Canaanites.

In this time, God raised up judges to redeem Israel from political slavery and give them an opportunity to repent. Israel often did repent for a single generation, but fell back into idolatry and disobedience, prompting once again God's wrath. Deborah was the only named female judge during this time.

She aggressively pulled on the moral bridle of Israel to return to worship of the one true God, and ruthlessly purified the nation of those evil actors who were interested in keeping Israel spiritually complacent and under slavery to the Canaanites.

The top Bible verse about Deborah:

"Certainly I will go with you," said Deborah. "But because of the course you are taking, the honor will not be yours, for the Lord will deliver Sisera into the hands of a woman" (Judg. 4:9).

8. Esther

Esther was a persecuting citizen of Israel under Persian reign. In the 7th–6th century BC, Esther was chosen out of the women of Israel to be part of the harem of King Xerxes. She used her political influence to destroy the antisemitic actors who sought to destroy the Jews in Persia, and through her faithfulness, established the Jewish festival of Purim. She was thereafter chosen by Xerxes to be his queen, and she ruled Israel as a Jewish queen of a gentile nation.

Like Deborah a thousand years earlier, Esther saved Israel from the consequences of its own spiritual folly and established a safe place for Jews to worship in the land. It was on this basis that Judaism was allowed to flourish under Greek and Roman rule in the centuries to come, and it was because of Esther that the ministry of Jesus was able to thrive freely and openly in a public society.

Simple story of Esther:

"So Queen Esther, daughter of Abigail, along with Mordecai the Jew, wrote with full authority to confirm this second letter concerning Purim. And Mordecai sent letters to all the Jews in the 127 provinces of Xerxes' kingdom words of goodwill and assurance to establish these days of Purim at their designated times, as Mordecai the Jew and Queen Esther had decreed for them, and as they had established for themselves and their descendants in regard to their times of fasting and lamentation" (Esther 9:29–31).

9. Miriam

Miriam was a prophetess and Moses's older sister. She helped to save Moses when he was only an infant. Moses's mother left him in a basket to protect him from being murdered by Pharaoh due to his being a Jewish baby. When Pharaoh's daughter found Moses and had mercy on him, Miriam devoted herself to Pharaoh's daughter in order to raise him so that they could remain together.

We can credit Miriam with instilling Moses with a devotion to the Lord that manifested itself in later days, which enabled his openness to divine encounter with the one true God and his moral conscience which guided Israel all the way to the promised land.

Miriam in the Bible:
"Then Miriam the prophet, Aaron's sister, took a timbrel in her hand, and all the women followed her, with timbrels and dancing. Miriam sang to them: "Sing to the LORD, for he is highly exalted. Both horse and driver he has hurled into the sea."" (Ex. 15:20–21)

10. Sarah
She was Abraham's wife, and served as an example of the fact that God always keeps his promises. When God promised Abraham, he would bear a son, despite Sarah's inability to bear children, Sarah gave birth to Isaac when she was 90-years old.

Sarah in the Bible:
"And God said, Sarah thy wife shall bear thee a son indeed; and thou shalt call his name Isaac: and I will establish my covenant with him for an everlasting covenant, [and] with his seed after him" (Gen. 17:19).

11. Elizabeth
Like Sarah, Elizabeth was far too old to conceive a son. However, God made it possible for her to bear a child. She would go on to conceive and give birth to John the Baptist, the last "Old Testament" prophet who would bear direct witness to the divinity and messianic authority of Jesus Christ.
Elizabeth's faithfulness is meant to draw our minds back to Sarah and the thousands of years during which Israel waited for the Messiah to come.

Elizabeth in the Bible:
"And when Elizabeth heard the greeting of Mary, the baby leaped in her womb. And Elizabeth was filled with the Holy Spirit" (Luke 1:41).

12. Priscilla
Priscilla was a powerful church leader in the book of Acts. She and her husband, Aquila, led the church in maintaining theological purity, love for the poor, and mentorship of young, charismatic leaders such Apollos, who were still figuring out how Jesus fit into God's story of redemption.
Priscilla represents God's counter-cultural insistence upon the dignity of women in church leadership and the power he plans to accomplish through them to revolutionize what it means to belong in the people of God and what women can do to lead by example in faithfulness and hospitality.

Priscilla in the Bible:

"He began to speak boldly in the synagogue. When Priscilla and Aquila heard him, they invited him to their home and explained to him the way of God more adequately" (Acts

18:26).

13. Mary of Bethany

Mary of Bethan was the sister of Martha and Lazarus, whom Jesus raised from the lead (Lazarus). She hosted Jesus in her home. While hosting him there, Jesus commended her for "choosing the better" by sitting at his feet instead of being distracted by housework and the duties of entertaining. Mary of Bethany represents Jesus's clear message that he cuts through cultural expectations and desires to extend fellowship to all human beings, despite the hierarchy humans are often tempted to put into place which marginalize and suppress others.

Mary of Bethany in the Bible:

"Six days before the Passover, Jesus therefore came to Bethany, where Lazarus was, whom Jesus had raised from the dead. So, they gave a dinner for him there. Martha served, and Lazarus was one of those reclining with him at table. Mary therefore took a pound[a] of expensive ointment made from pure nard, and anointed the feet of Jesus and wiped his feet with her hair. The house was filled with the fragrance of the perfume. But Judas Iscariot, one of his disciples (he who was about to betray him), said, 'Why was this ointment not sold for three hundred denarii[b] and given to the poor?' He said this, not because he cared about the poor, but because he was a thief, and having charge of the moneybag he used to help himself to what was put into it. Jesus said, 'Leave her alone, so that she may keep it for the day of my burial. For the poor you always have with you, but you do not always have me' (John 12:1-8).

14. Martha

Mary's sister Martha was rebuked by Jesus for putting her entertainment obligations above learning the words of Jesus. However, she was still a devoted disciple of Christ and desired deeply to know and love Jesus, and did everything in her power to dignify him as the unknown king.

Martha in the Bible:

"Now as they went on their way, Jesus entered a village. And a woman named Martha welcomed him into her house. And she had a sister called Mary, who sat at the Lord's feet and listened to his teaching. But Martha was distracted with much serving. And she went up to him and said, ‘Lord, do you not care that my sister has left me to serve alone? Tell her then to help me.’ But the Lord answered her, ‘Martha, Martha, you are anxious and troubled about many things, but one thing is necessary. Mary has chosen the good portion, which will not be taken away from her’” (Luke 10:38–42).

A biblical account of the woman from Shunem

[8] One day Elisha went to Shunem, where a rich woman lived. She invited him to a meal, and
from then on, every time he went to Shunem he would have his meals at her house. [9] She said
to her husband, “I am sure that this man who comes here so often is a holy man. [10] Let's build
a small room on the roof, put a bed, a table, a chair, and a lamp in it, and he can stay there
whenever he visits us.”

[11] One day Elisha returned to Shunem and went up to his room to rest. [12] He told his servant
Gehazi to go and call the woman. When she came, [13] he said to Gehazi, “Ask her what I can do
for her in return for all the trouble she has had in providing for our needs. Maybe she would
like me to go to the king or the army commander and put in a good word for her.”

“I have all I need here among my own people,” she answered.

[14] Elisha asked Gehazi, “What can I do for her then? He answered, “Well, she has no son, and
her husband is an old man.”

[15] “Tell her to come here,” Elisha ordered. She came and stood in the doorway, [16] and Elisha
said to her, “By this time next year you will be holding a son in your arms.”

“Oh!” she exclaimed. “Please, sir, don't lie to me. You are a man of God!”

[17] But, as Elisha had said, at about that time the following year she gave birth to a son.

[18] Some years later, at harvest time, the boy went out one morning to join his father, who was
in the field with the harvest workers. [19] Suddenly he cried out to his father, “My head hurts!
My head hurts!”

“Carry the boy to his mother,” the father said to a servant. [20] The servant carried the boy back
to his mother, who held him in her lap until noon, at which time he died. [21] She carried him up
to Elisha's room, put him on the bed and left, closing the door behind her. [22] Then she called

her husband and said to him, “Send a servant here with a donkey. I need to go to the prophet Elisha. I'll be back as soon as I can.”

23 “Why do you have to go today?” her husband asked. “It's neither a Sabbath nor a New Moon Festival.”

“Never mind,” she answered. 24 Then she had the donkey saddled, and ordered the servant, “Make the donkey go as fast as it can, and don't slow down unless I tell you to.” 25 So she set out and went to Mount Carmel, where Elisha was.

Elisha saw her coming while she was still some distance away, and he said to his servant Gehazi, “Look, there comes the woman from Shunem! 26 Hurry to her and find out if everything is all right with her, her husband, and her son.”

She told Gehazi that everything was all right, 27 but when she came to Elisha, she bowed down before him and took hold of his feet. Gehazi was about to push her away, but Elisha said, “Leave her alone. Can't you see she's deeply distressed? And the LORD has not told me a thing about it.”

28 The woman said to him, “Sir, did I ask you for a son? Didn't I tell you not to get my hopes up?”

29 Elisha turned to Gehazi and said, “Hurry! Take my walking stick and go. Don't stop to greet anyone you meet, and if anyone greets you, don't take time to answer. Go straight to the house and hold my stick over the boy.”

30 The woman said to Elisha, “I swear by my loyalty to the living LORD and to you that I will not leave you!” So, the two of them started back together. 31 Gehazi went on ahead and held Elisha's stick over the child, but there was no sound or any other sign of life. So, he went back to meet Elisha and said, “The boy didn't wake up.”

32 When Elisha arrived, he went alone into the room and saw the boy lying dead on the bed. 33 He closed the door and prayed to the LORD. 34 Then he lay down on the boy, placing his mouth, eyes, and hands on the boy's mouth, eyes, and hands. As he lay stretched out over the boy, the boy's body started to get warm. 35 Elisha got up, walked around the room, and then went back and again stretched himself over the boy. The boy sneezed seven times and then

opened his eyes. [36] Elisha called Gehazi and told him to call the boy's mother. When she came in, he said to her, "Here's your son." [37] She fell at Elisha's feet, with her face touching the ground; then she took her son and left.

Jesus Was Funded by Rich Women (Casey Graham, March 2011)

I can't believe this passage of Scripture isn't taught more or studied deeper. This is one of the clearest passages about Jesus and his ministry being funded. Soon afterward Jesus began a tour of the nearby towns and villages, preaching and announcing the Good News about the Kingdom of God. He took his twelve disciples with him, along with some women who had been cured of evil spirits and diseases. Among them were Mary Magdalene, from whom he had cast out seven demons, Joanna, the wife of Chuza, Herod's business manager, Susanna, and many others who were contributing their own resources to support Jesus and his disciples. (Luke 8: 1-3)

Let's look at some key points that apply to your ministry:

1. The Women Who Gave Had Been "Cured of Evil Spirits and Diseases"

People fund ministries where they find Jesus, and he radically changes their lives. This is why it is so important to be Gospel centred, not financially centred, in your church. If Jesus changes their lives, it is EASY to make the ask.

2. Women Give More than Men

This Scripture is very clear that women were funding his ministry at a high level. Check out this study done on the generosity level of women. Women are statistically more generous than men. If this is true, why do we leave them out a lot of times when having meetings about funding the vision? Never have a fund-raising conversation of significance with JUST the husband. Include the spouse always! Very important.

3. The People Who Funded the Ministry Were CLOSE to Jesus

What can we learn from the text when it says, "He took his twelve disciples, along with some women"?

Jesus had many people in his ministry ask if they could go on the journey with him, and he told them no. He had people that he told them to just go back to their town. Why would Jesus invite these women on the journey and then the text point this out?

I believe it's a super clear passage showing the importance of cultivating relationships with High-Capacity Donors. He could have said, "No, you can't come; just send your money." Jesus gave these ladies access to his life, and they funded because of their lives being changed and being included. Was Jesus "showing favouritism" by knowing what they gave and having his donors on the journey? NO, he was modelling the way!

What do you think about this text? Anything we can learn about funding that I missed?

Casey Graham is the founder of The Rocket Company. He worked for ten years in the trenches of local church ministry, which led to his passion for helping church leaders win in their ministry and personal lives. He lives in Atlanta, Georgia with his wife, kids and their Westie dog named Westie.

Women Workers in the New Testament

People everywhere have always worked. And when we turn to the New Testament we find women engaged in all kinds of employment. For some it was the work of bearing and rearing children. For others it was bringing aid to folks in need. And for still others it was as businesswomen engaged in profitable enterprises. For many it was some form of ministry for Christ and his kingdom.

Women Happily Accept Significant Work (Luke 1)

When we open the Gospel according to Luke, we immediately meet an elderly woman named Elizabeth, the wife of a Jewish priest, and a young girl named Mary, engaged to marry a carpenter. Barren Elizabeth is now six months pregnant in her old age and will later give birth to John the Baptist. Mary, likely in her early teens, is also pregnant, but uniquely by God's Spirit, not by sex with any man. After her encounter with God's angel and her agreement to become the mother of God's Messiah, Mary journeys on foot the seventy miles from the province of Galilee in the north to the highlands of Judea to visit her cousin Elizabeth. For both women their pregnancies were supernatural.

We may not think of bearing and rearing children as "work" and wonder why an article on women in the workplace should begin with two pregnant women. But in both cases, these women were partnering in God's work to invade a broken and sinful world and reverse the grip of evil on people's lives. This partnership required real work. There would be physical work in bearing and rearing these special boys, to be sure. But Mary and Elizabeth embraced the prospect of this work joyfully. Mary captured the significance God intended for her work in her song that we call the Magnificat:

My soul magnifies the Lord, and my spirit rejoices in God my Savior. For he has looked with favor on the lowliness of his servant...He has shown strength with his arm; he has scattered the proud in the thoughts of their hearts. He has brought down the powerful from their thrones, and lifted up the lowly; he has filled the hungry with good things, and sent the rich away empty. (Luke 1:46-53)

Giving birth was not the only meaningful work Mary did in her lifetime. She also played a role in Jesus' adult ministry. Yet the part of her story that inspires us today is how she trusted God's purposes despite the difficult work it would mean for her.

Women Make Jesus' Work Possible (Luke 4:14-19)

Back to Table of Contents

Jesus, now in his thirties, "filled with the power of the Spirit, returned to Galilee, and a report about him spread through all the surrounding country. He began to teach in their synagogues and was praised by everyone" (Luke 4:14-15). Going throughout Galilee's cities and villages proclaiming God's Good News (Luke 4:18-19), "the twelve [male disciples] were with him as well as some women who had been cured of evil spirits and infirmities: Mary, called Magdalene, from whom seven demons had gone out, and Joanna, the wife of Herod's steward Chuza, and Susanna, and many others, who provided for them out of their resources" (Luke 8:1-3).

These women, healed in some way by Jesus, were part of that traveling band following the Lord around Galilee. The women's self-appointed work was to care for Jesus' physical needs in his travels. Given the patriarchal society of first-century Palestine in which women were most often sequestered, have you ever wondered how these women could travel with Jesus and his followers without creating any hint of scandal? The fact that they had wealth made them benefactors with the freedom to come and go in public without being censured. If you've ever wondered how Jesus and his followers could survive for three years without an obvious source of income, look no further than to these wealthy women.

Jesus' Teachings Include Women

Back to Table of Contents

The four gospel accounts of Jesus' earthly ministry contain the mention of more women than virtually any other secular writing of that era. In them we hear Jesus praise women for their faith (the Canaanite woman in Matthew 15:28; Martha in John 11:26-27) or for their generosity (a poor widow's gift, Mark 12:43-44). He included them in his teachings (about a woman baking bread, Matthew 13:33; or a woman hunting for a lost coin, Luke 15:8-10). Contrary to custom, he spoke freely to women in public (John 8:10-11) and taught theology to them (Luke 10:39). He entrusted them with the message of the resurrection while the male disciples hid in fear of the Jewish authorities.

In contrast to some of the disciples, no woman deserted him, betrayed him, or failed to believe his words. Because of their faith, their understanding, and their fidelity, women were often examples to the men. And after his ascension to God's heaven, these same faithful women were with the men in prayer in an upper room in Jerusalem, waiting for the promise of God's Spirit to prepare them for ongoing ministry.

Some folks suggest that because we don't hear of these women later in the New Testament, they were never more than benefactors to Jesus in his earthly ministry. But neither do we hear of all but two of the disciples in the rest of the New Testament. Yet we know the strong tradition that Thomas went to India as an evangelist and church-planter. We assume that all of them (except the suicide Judas) scattered in every direction, carrying the Gospel of Jesus to the ends of the known earth.

The book of Acts carries, initially, the work of Peter as leader of the early church in Jerusalem (with the baton soon passed to James, the brother of Jesus, not James the disciple). Then the story picks up with the apostle Paul, working sometimes with Barnabas, sometimes with Silas. And it is here that we find the fascinating stories of women in a variety of professions who became followers of Jesus and ardent workers in the new churches scattered around the Roman Empire.

This is the true story of five working women, whose original professions were totally diverse, but who ended up in the same surprising position. Our authority for their stories is the apostle Paul. We find their stories in two places: in Luke's account of the early Christian churches, in particular as he traveled with the apostle Paul, then in the letters of the apostle.

The Businesswoman Lydia (Acts 16)

Back to Table of Contents

Our first story is about a woman in the northwest Turkish town of Thyatira, known for its guilds of craftsmen, especially the guild of the professionals knowledgeable in the production and sale of expensive purple dye. Lydia was a member of that guild. We don't know how it was that a woman had become one of those professionals, but when we first meet her, she had crossed into northeastern Greece and had established her business base in the Roman city of Philippi. As a seller of rare and expensive purple dye, Lydia must have had enough wealth to buy into that franchise.

We learn in Acts 16 that, while born and reared to believe in the gods and goddesses of Thyatira, Lydia did not worship the pantheon of gods venerated in her hometown. Instead, she had become a "God-fearer." She had already taken a major step away from her religious upbringing and had investigated Jewish claims of one God and wanted to know more. (Many God-fearers became Jewish proselytes.) We first meet her at Philippi's riverside with a group of women who had come together there to pray. It was there that Paul and Silas met her and talked with her about Jesus, and there she became the first convert to Christianity in Greece.

Convinced of the truth of the Christian gospel and believing that it was for everyone, she bore witness to her entire household and with her, they were all baptized. The apostles stayed on with her for several weeks, instructing her and her household in what she needed as a new follower of Jesus. There in her large house she began the first Christian church on Greek soil, welcoming other new believers into the fellowship of faith.

Lydia was successful both in her professional work and in her social or spiritual work nurturing the nascent Greek church. Most likely the knowledge and connections she cultivated as a trader helped her in her church work, and vise versa. In Lydia we see a woman whose skill and interest is not confined to one limited area. Indeed, we see that both her position in commerce and her knowledge of faith made her uniquely qualified to spearhead the church in Greece.

The Intellectual Damaris (Acts 17:17)

As the apostle Paul continued his ministry in various Greek cities, he ended up one day in the unique city Athens, known for its university and its intellectual climate. In Acts 17 we watch him wandering through the city, astonished by all the idols and shrines to an endless list of gods and goddesses. We read in Acts 17:17 that "he began to interact with the Jews and Gentile God-worshippers in the synagogue. He also addressed whoever happened to be in the marketplace each day. Certain Epicurean and Stoic philosophers engaged him in discussion." Out of that he received an invitation to address the Aeropaus, the leading council of Athens. As he spoke of Jesus, some ridiculed him, but others believed. Among the believers was a woman named Damaris.

In the culture of that city, women lived sequestered lives. But one group of women was exempt from that. These were the intellectual courtesans, high-class prostitutes attached to rich men in the city. These women were able to hold their own intellectually, carrying on esoteric debates on philosophical subjects. The Bible doesn't tell us specifically that Damaris was a courtesan, but the fact that she was allowed to be present at Paul's meeting with the leading men of the city strongly indicates that possibility. Both her freedom to be in public and her ability to follow Paul's conversation with the leading men enabled her to understand and to embrace the gospel Paul taught. She became one of the new converts to Christianity in the city of Athens.

New Testament scholar Richard Bauckham tells us that any time we come across the name of someone in the book of Acts or in the apostle's letters, it's there because that person had become widely known among the Christian churches as teacher and leader. Because we know Damaris's name, we also know that she was well-known for ministry in the churches. As an intellectual herself, she had the ability to reach the intelligentsia in Athens.

If Damaris began her career as a high-class escort and ended it as an evangelist, we might wonder what change this brought to her income, influence, or working conditions. The answers might be lost to history. At the very least we can say that God may lead a woman to change careers, and he certainly entrusts important work to women from a diversity of backgrounds.

The Businesswoman Phoebe (Romans 16:1-2)

The apostle Paul left Athens and moved on to Corinth. This city was radically different from Athens. Located on the narrow neck of land joining a large southern peninsula to the mainland of Greece, Corinth had two ports: one on the west coast on the Adriatic Sea and one on the east coast on the Saronic Gulf. A Roman city (like Philippi) in Greece, it was a bustling commercial city with a very diverse ethnic population and a plethora of temples to every known god or goddess (including Egyptian deities). Once in Corinth Paul settled down for eighteen months, preaching and starting new Christian churches.

It's there that we meet Phoebe. While in Corinth Paul had written a long letter to the Christians in the city of Rome, and he needed someone to carry the letter to them. It appears that Phoebe travelled for business purposes and offered to take the letter on her next trip to Rome. So, we meet her in Paul's letter where he describes her to the Christians in Rome:

I commend to you our sister Phoebe, a deacon of the church in Cenchreae so that you may welcome her in the Lord as is fitting for the saints, and help her in whatever she may require from you, for she has been a benefactor of many and of myself as well (Romans 16:1-2).

Note the two words Paul used to describe her. In the church she was, first, a deacon, a term Paul uses for only five people in his letters: himself, Tychicus, Epaphras, Timothy, and Phoebe. Whatever he and the other three men were doing as deacons, we can assume that Phoebe was also doing in the churches.

But Paul then uses a second word to describe her. Our translation (NRSV) calls her a "benefactor," but the Greek word in Paul's letter was prostatis. According to the lexicographer Thayer, the first meaning of that word was "a woman set over others." The Greek word was in the feminine form of the masculine word prostates, usually translated leader. It referred to "one who preaches, teaches, and presides at the Lord's Table." Obviously, Phoebe, the business woman was more than merely a benefactor. She was a leader of the church in Cenchreae.

Like the businesswoman Lydia, Phoebe used her wealth and influence to grow the Christian church. She even leveraged a business trip to spread the gospel. But she didn't just carry a man's message. Phoebe was a church leader in her own right. Today, women are often denied equal responsibility both in businesses and in churches. However, this was not the precedent set by the earliest Christian churches.

The Tentmaker Priscilla (Acts 18:2)

In Corinth Paul needed a means to support himself, and fortunately, he had a trade: he made leather tents for the Roman government and private parties who ordered them. Once in Corinth, he collaborated with a couple who also made leather tents: Priscilla and Aquila. (The Roman government required leather tents for housing its military on bases all over the empire. A canvas tent would not do, especially in northern climates. Furthermore, Paul could carry with him the few tools for leatherwork, but would not have been able to carry necessary equipment for working with canvas. Canvas was usually used for boat sails.)

While scholars believe that Priscilla was a Gentile (and from the Roman aristocracy), she had married Aquila, a Jew from the Turkish province of Pontus. They lived in Rome and were part of the folks who worked with the apostle Peter in his evangelism there. But the Roman emperor (around 51-52 A.D.) ordered that all Jews be expelled from Rome. Corinth was the nearest major city outside Italy, so as refugees, they had settled there. And there they connected with the apostle Paul.

This tentmaking couple became so valuable to the apostle Paul that when he left Corinth to begin missionary work in Ephesus, he took Priscilla and Aquila with him. This couple is mentioned six times in the New Testament, and in all but one case, Priscilla's name is given first. This wasn't simply a matter of courtesy in the first century; it indicated her primacy in their work together. Eventually, when the exile of Jews from Rome was lifted, they returned to their home in the capital city and once again became active in starting new churches there.

Priscilla is often thought of as a tentmaker, but clearly, she was many other things in her lifetime too: a businesswoman, a refugee, a traveling evangelist, and a church planter. While we often hear stories about complex men in the Bible, in Priscilla we see that women too are multitalented, multifaceted, and capable of working in a variety of different environments.

The Jewish Palace Insider and Benefactor Junia (Romans 16:6)

Biblical scholars have puzzled over the years about Paul's reference in Romans 16:6: "Greet Andronicus and Junia, my relatives who were in prison with me; they are prominent among the apostles, and they were in Christ before I was." Who were these folks? Paul was clear that they were related to him, that they had shared prison time with him, they were prominent apostles, and they had become believers before he had. Who could fill that bill?

That points to someone who was Jewish, had known Jesus in his earthly ministry (the requirement for the title apostle), and had signed on as a Jesus-follower before Paul himself. Now they were in Rome.

In his book Gospel Women, noted biblical scholar Richard Bauckham untangles the knots in this mystery for us, starting with one of the women healed by Jesus, mentioned in Luke 8:3. She was Joanna, the wife of Chuza, the business manager for king Herod Antipas. It turns out that the name Joanna is the Hebrew equivalent of the Roman name Junia. Could Joanna in the gospels be the same person as the apostle Junia? Look at some of the possible clues leading to that conclusion.

The name Chuza is not a Jewish name, and he is thought to have been Nabatean (King Herod Antipas had other connections to the Nabatean royal family). But as the king's finance minister living in the new Roman-style palace in the royal city of Tiberias, he needed a Jewish wife connected to a wealthy Jewish family. Enter young Joanna (probably just entering puberty when she was married to the much older, mature man, Chuza). While king Herod Antipas had some Jewish blood, his kingship depended on Rome, so palace life in Tiberias followed Roman practices. Joanna would likely have been given a Roman name (Junia) and would have been formed in Roman ways of acting and thinking.

We first meet Joanna in the Bible, however, not as part of the royal household, but as a woman in need of healing. Luke tells us that after Jesus healed her, she became part of his traveling band of women caring for the physical needs of the Saviour. In short, she became one of his benefactors, providing funds for the support of his group.

What the Bible does not tell us is whether or not Chuza had died and Joanna was widowed, but scholars surmise this likely was the case (given the probable disparity in their ages). Nor does the Bible tell us that in traveling with Jesus' band, she might eventually have remarried, becoming the wife of Andrew, one of Jesus's disciples. If, however, this was the case, it would answer to all of the clues given in Paul's greeting to this couple in Romans 16:6. We know that Peter first carried the Gospel to Rome, and to bring along his brother and fellow disciple, Andrew, is logical. So as Paul's letter to the Romans was read to the assembled Christians, he addressed this apostolic pair by their Roman names – Andronicus and Junia.

Paul doesn't tell us that back in Palestine they had been Andrew and Joanna, but all of his clues fit that possibility.

Pinpointing the identity of Junia leads us through some fascinating detective work. It is unfortunate though that we often have to struggle to uncover the significant work of women throughout history. In all fields of human achievement, the contributions of women have often been either swept under the rug, or ascribed to males whom we see as more likely sources of innovation, intelligence, or heroism. Women still struggle to be acknowledged for their work. And yet, God has always seen the value of women workers. Throughout the New Testament God chose women as well as men to understand his message and to work for his purposes.

Women Workers in the New Testament

Women as well as men were leaders in those first-century churches. That practice was a radical departure from pagan philosophical notions accepted at that time. So, the wider culture began pushing back against women leaders in the churches. Centuries earlier, Aristotle had taught that a woman was a "failed male" with a "flawed anatomy." She should not lead. One by one, the later Church Fathers imbibed Aristotle's idea and began closing the door to leadership for women. By the third century, women were effectively locked out of any kind of Christian leadership.

But that did not stamp out the first-century vision of men and women working side-by-side in ministry. We have their record in the New Testament, in the stories of Mary, Mary Magdalene, Lydia, Damaris, Phoebe, Pricilla, and Junia. From these stories we can reconstruct a history of women working both in the church and in the marketplace for God's purposes. Thanks be to God.

Introduction

God intends for everyone to thrive economically. He wants us to find provision (basic needs) for our daily life. He also desires for us to enjoy the wealth (abundance) of his generosity. Furthermore, God's world has ample resources to provide all we need. However, in the fallen world we inhabit, many people do not experience God's abundant provision. Others find their needs are met, but only at great cost (emotional, physical, relational, environmental, moral or spiritual) to themselves and those around them. Then there are still other people who attain significant economic wealth, but this is gained through harming others or themselves. Whatever situation we find ourselves in economically, questions and concerns about God's intent and role in provision and wealth weigh heavily on almost every Christian's mind. Such matters are to the fore in the lives of rich and poor; employer, employee and job seeker; student, parent and retiree; homeowner, tenant and homeless person.

Fortunately, this concern for the economic is matched by the priority it is given in Scripture. Indeed, provision and wealth are far from peripheral issues in the Bible. They occupy a large share of both the Old and New Testaments, and are prominent in the Gospels.

So what does God's word have to say to us? In this article we will explore:

- God's original intentions for us regarding provision and wealth
- The impact living in a fallen world has had on our capacity to experience provision and wealth
- God's response in redeeming the economic sphere, and our role in this
- What we can reasonably expect from God in regard to our provision
- How we should treat any wealth we possess

Overall, our emphasis is more on God's intent for how we handle wealth, and less on what it means to depend on God for basic provision. Many who read this article may feel anxious about whether God will provide for their needs, but we guess that for the majority of readers, much of the anxiety is really about whether they will continue to enjoy a high level of wealth—by world standards—rather than basic provision. Basic provision is nonetheless an essential part of the discussion, of course, and we welcome further insight in this area, especially from those whose experience in living with poverty and anxiety about basic provision is greater than ours.

God's Original Intentions: Blessing, Provision, Abundance

The account of Genesis 1 and 2 makes it clear that God planned for humanity to enjoy the beauty, abundance and fruitfulness of creation. In the idyllic setting of the Garden of Eden, the first humans found a rich, fertile place, and humanity was intended to prosper in every sense. God provides an abundance of resources and means for humans to flourish.

As the writer of Genesis states early on in the story about the creation of humans, "God blessed them" (Genesis 1:28). The word "blessing" or "blessed" is a central feature of the biblical story. Part of the blessing of relationship with God is very definitely tangible, in-the-hand stuff. And these material blessings are thoroughly integrated with the other benefits of knowing and loving the Creator.

Later, even in the barrenness of the wilderness, the people of Israel find daily provision from God, in the form of manna (Exodus 16) and water gushing from the rock (Exodus 17). The abundant wealth of God's creation is discovered further on in the biblical narrative by the people of Israel, when they finally reach the Promised Land. It is a land "flowing with milk and honey," rich with all the ingredients needed to live according to God's design. Deuteronomy records the promise made to God's people in the desert that they would find on earth everything they need to prosper.

For the Lord your God is bringing you into a good land, a land with flowing streams, with springs and underground waters welling up in valleys and hills, a land of wheat and barley, of vines and fig trees and pomegranates, a land of olive trees and honey, a land where you may eat bread without scarcity, where you will lack nothing. (Deuteronomy 8:7-9)

From the beginning, God perfectly provisioned the world for humans to thrive. The good earth yields food when humans exercise their God-given ability to "till it and keep it" (Genesis 2:15). God's intent is that people would not merely subsist, but have good things in abundance. "Be fruitful and multiply, and fill the earth and subdue it" (Genesis 1:28). God gives people the capacity to understand the natural world so that we make use of its resources (Genesis 2:20). Human work and ingenuity are more than capable of developing God's creation to provide abundantly for all people. In partnership with the Creator, we are to make creative use of the resources of the earth, growing and innovating, creating new products, improving on the original. There is more than enough raw material to go around. This is in stark contrast to the principle of scarcity that applies to most goods and materials in post-Eden economics.

At our best, we humans have cooperated with God amazingly well in developing his creation. Whether it be the development of agriculture and horticulture, the harnessing of coal, oil, gas, wind and water for power generation, the creation of parks, gardens and images of beauty, or the design and building of houses, appliances, clothes and modes of transport, all such developments that enrich our lives are expressions of co-creation. The capacity to innovate, produce and develop is part of what it means to be made in God's image.

The Effects of a Fallen World

The rebellion of the first humans (Genesis 3) had a catastrophic effect on all of creation—not just their relationship with God, but also their capacity to draw provision and create wealth from the land. The Fall demonstrates that when we break our relationship with God, we create economic problems, along with all sorts of other evil. Because God is the source of blessing, no longer being close to him undermines humanity's ability to find provision and wealth.

As a result of the Fall, people began to live under both a curse and a blessing. This had significant implications for work. The land—and therefore its productivity and fruitfulness—is deeply impaired by the breaking of relationship, prompting God to say to Adam:

Cursed is the ground because of you; in toil you shall eat of it all the days of your life; thorns and thistles it shall bring forth for you; and you shall eat the plants of the field. By the sweat of your face you shall eat bread until you return to the ground… (Genesis 3:17b-19a)

We may even become unable to draw basic provision from the materials of creation, whether by our own fault, or by the fault of others, or by no one's fault in particular. Drug abuse, poor work habits, lack of access to education, ill health, concentration of resources in the hands of elites, ethnic discrimination and a myriad of other causes may prevent individuals, families, communities, and entire societies from co-creation with God of the provision they need. In the fallen world we inhabit, God's original intentions for provision and wealth are disrupted in several notable ways.

Many People Are Unable to Obtain Even Basic Provision

About 1.4 billion of the world's population live in extreme poverty, meaning they lack the basic necessities of life. A further 1.1 billion live at subsistence level, on a kind of "hand-to-mouth" existence that is only one crisis away from disaster.[1] Economic poverty affects nearly 40 percent of humanity. Given what we have seen in Genesis 1 and 2, this is clearly not how God intended things to be. So why is this the daily reality of so many people?

In a world that was entirely level and fair, good choices would lead to provision and wealth, and poor choices to poverty. In such a cause-and-effect world, the truth of proverbs such as, "In all toil there is profit, but mere talk leads only to poverty," (Proverbs 14:23) would make perfect sense. Laziness, wasteful indulgence, poor self-discipline and addictive behaviour would all lead naturally to poverty. On the other hand, hard work, careful consumption, healthy self-discipline and freedom from addictions would result in wealth. This may be the case for millions or billions of people in the world today—their relative wealth or poverty being due largely to their own good choices, hard work, and ingenuity. In well-governed societies, among those with equal access to resources and education, and in situations where illness, disaster, family dysfunction, crime, and accidents do not hamper people, individuals' wealth and poverty may be the fair outcomes of personal effort.

But the truth is that on a global scale, we don't live in anything close to a level playing field. The fallen world is neither fair nor even-handed. None of us start life from the same position. Our family, community and societal circumstances dictate much about our opportunities in the world. Some of us are fortunate to be born into loving, nurturing families in prosperous countries, with a myriad of abilities and opportunities. Sadly, others are born into circumstances that are resourceless in every sense of the word. They are never given the basis they need to provide for themselves.

It is true that the majority of poverty is a result of some form of human sin and error. But it is not necessarily *their own sin* that causes people to lack provision or wealth. Poor government, war, corruption, exploitation by the powerful, lack of education and training, family and social ills that prevent people from reaching their potential, all contribute to many people not having enough, through no fault of their own. In particular, lack of provision often lies in whole or part with social or personal sin *against* the poor. That is, they are victims of others' sin. A tyrant confiscates a family's land, depriving them of their capacity to produce. A factory exploits vulnerable workers by paying below legal wages and threatening those who object. A wealthy landowner strips large tracts of forested land of its vegetation, putting millions of people downstream at risk of flooding. A husband becomes addicted to gambling, and leaves his wife and children penniless. An investment fails because of fraud and deception, leaving a family who had saved hard for the future without means.

Even so, not all poverty is the result of sin, or at least not sin that can be traced to anyone in particular. Some people are unable to provide for their needs because of disability, illness, age or other factors that aren't anyone's fault. In the Old Testament, three such groups of people were particularly vulnerable—"the widow, the orphan and the foreigner."[2] Anticipating this, the Hebrew Law contained regulations that would ensure these people were provided for.[3] Zechariah is typical of the Prophets when he writes: "Thus says the Lord of hosts: Render true judgments, show kindness and mercy to one another; do not oppress the widow, the orphan, the alien, or the poor" (Zechariah 7:9-10).[4]

Other poverty occurs because of the unpredictability of our planet. A natural disaster such as an earthquake, tsunami, drought or flood can devastate whole communities, destroying crops, homes, possessions and livelihoods in a single moment. For example, a quarter of a million people lost their lives in the Boxing Day tsunami in 2004 that swamped coastal Indonesia and other parts of South East Asia, and many more survivors were left homeless and without any means to provide for themselves.

We must be very careful then, not to make assumptions about the reasons for anyone's situation—rich or poor. So many factors are at work, some of individuals' own making; many outside their control. The Bible is very realistic in this regard. For example, it has been noted that, "fewer than one-third of the proverbs dealing with rich and poor teach that people get what they deserve, whereas the rest recognize the presence and problem of socio-economic justice."[5] So while there are times when the Bible connects provision or lack of it with a cause, generally Scripture is less concerned with identifying the particular causes of poverty and more concerned with the obligations of those who have wealth to care for those who lack provision.

Many People Find Provision and Even Become Wealthy—But Cause Great Harm

Earning Money at All Cost Is a Strategy That's Bad for My Soul (Click to Watch)

Compared to the billions of people who struggle to scratch out a daily existence, those in the world who have enough to satisfy their needs and more may seem blessed. And they are, economically speaking, at least. However, having plenty can come at the cost of great harm to the individual, family, community or nation that has it and also to those who may suffer as a consequence. We will explore several situations of provision or wealth causing harm to those who gain it or those they exploit to do so.

Wealth Gained Through Unjust Means Is Harmful

Some national leaders attain provision or wealth through unjust means such as exploitation, force, corruption, theft and others. Brutal dictators and regimes take what they want, oppressing their own people through force and intimidation, living lives of luxury while their people struggle to survive. Burma, Zimbabwe, Libya…the list could go on.

Some multi-national corporations exploit cheap labour markets, impose unsafe working conditions on desperate workers, or devastate local ecosystems in order to reap outsized profits. Their gains occur at great cost to people and places unseen by home-country regulators and disconnected from the consumers who buy the products.

Some individuals and organizations defraud or deceive household investors into taking excessive risks, without any concern for the people they might be hurting in the process.

These are just a few of the ways wealth is obtained to the detriment of others. The cause of such injustices is so often greed—"an intense and selfish desire for wealth, power or food."[6] The Apostle Paul confronts this issue in the church at Ephesus when he writes to Timothy, arguing that

Those who want to be rich fall into temptation and are trapped by many senseless and harmful desires that plunge people into ruin and destruction. For the love of money is a root of all kinds of evil, and in their eagerness to be rich some have wandered away from the faith and pierced themselves with many pains. (1 Timothy 6:9-10)

The consequences of such greed are often more than just damage to our own spiritual state and the deprivation of others economically. Greed can also produce degradation of the environment—resulting in significant damage to the earth, which ultimately affects the capacity of others to live well and reduces future productivity for everyone.

Sadly, in ancient Israel some people became rich through unjust means. In fact, much of the message of the Prophets targets economic injustice by those with wealth and power in Israel. Through spokespersons such as Amos, Micah and Jeremiah, God states that our worship is meaningless if we are accumulating wealth through the exploitation of others. If we say we love God, then this should be reflected in the way we treat others and conduct business.

Judgment comes on Israel, "because they sell the righteous for silver and the needy for a pair of sandals" (Amos 2:6b). Such condemnation is an inevitable consequence of the nation of Israel's failure to be faithful to its covenantal responsibilities. For God's trademarks are his steadfast love, justice and righteousness.[7] By implication, they are also core to what it means to be the covenant community. For ensuring that all members of society (and particularly the weak) have access to resources in order to live a life of dignity, is part of Israel's covenantal responsibilities.

Sadly, the mechanisms under the Law that sought to build a fair, just and compassionate society had been flouted and ignored. Instead of modeling God's shalom, Israel had become just like every other nation—a cesspit of oppression, abuse of power, and flagrant disregard for those caught on the economic scrapheap. The rich gained ownership of much of the land (in contravention of Leviticus 25:25-28), then leased it back to small farmers at interest (forbidden by Deuteronomy 23:19-20), which in turn led to default of loans. Meanwhile, they perverted the justice system by bribery. As a result, those dispossessed of capacity to earn a living had to sell themselves into slavery.

In response, the prophet Amos pleads, "Let justice roll down like waters, and righteousness like an everflowing stream" (Amos 5:24). Micah asks: "What does the Lord require of you but to do justice, and to love kindness, and to walk humbly with your God?" (Micah 6:8). The *way* we earn, employ or manage others, conduct business, invest and spend our money can be just *or* unjust. And this cannot be separated from our worship of God. We cannot love God and exploit other people in pursuit of wealth.

Legitimate Wealth Can Still Be Harmful

Not all accumulation of wealth is a result of injustice. However, even when wealth is gained through legitimate means, it still has the potential to do great harm. There are many passages of Scripture that alert the reader to the truth that wealth is dangerous. Riches can cause all kinds of negative side effects:

Firstly, wealth can lead to pride and arrogance. Proverbs 28:11 notes, "The rich is wise in self-esteem, but an intelligent poor person sees through the pose." It is easy for those with wealth to believe they have gained it solely through their own cleverness or hard work. Ezekiel warns the King of Tyre, "By your great wisdom in trade you have increased your wealth, and your heart has become proud in your wealth" (Ezekiel 28:5).

Secondly, wealth frequently leads to self-sufficiency, complacency and a false sense of security. One extreme example of this is Ephraim's boast in Hosea 12:8. "Ah, I am rich, I have gained wealth for myself; in all of my gain no offense has been found in me that would be sin." And the words of Hosea a chapter later are also very poignant—describing Israel's abandonment of God—"When I fed them, they were satisfied; they were satisfied, and their heart was proud" (Hosea 13:6). Jesus also notes the danger of wealth lulling us into a false sense of security, in his parable of the rich fool (Luke 12:13-21). It is only too easy to think that we have no need of God when our bellies are full, life is good, and the future seems assured.

Thirdly, wealth can also dull our senses to the deep needs around us, draining us of compassion and mercy. Jesus tells the parable of the rich man and Lazarus (Luke 16:19-31). Even though the poor man Lazarus lives in great distress at the rich man's gate, the rich man is impervious to his plight, so consumed is he with his own lifestyle and consumption. Ironically, even in Hades, the rich man is obsessed with his own needs and still views Lazarus as nothing but a pawn.

Fourthly, and most seductive of all, is the lure riches have in capturing our hearts and dividing our loyalties. Here we see the Bible's acknowledgment of the power that money wields. The Psalmist warns us of this when he writes, "If riches increase, do not set your heart on them" (Psalm 62:10b). This danger is also carefully spelled out for the people of Israel in Deuteronomy 8:12-17:

When you have eaten your fill and have built fine houses and live in them, and when your herds and flocks have multiplied, and your silver and gold is multiplied…then do not exalt yourself, forgetting the Lord your God…Do not say to yourself, "My power and the might of my own hand have gotten me this wealth."

These are sobering words. Perhaps this is why the writer of Proverbs 30 asks of God:

Give me neither poverty nor riches; feed me with the food that I need, or I shall be full, and deny you, and say, "Who is the Lord?" or I shall be poor, and steal, and profane the name of my God. (Proverbs 30:8-9)

The dangers of wealth are even more pronounced in the New Testament. Central to the attitude of Jesus is his statement:

No one can serve two masters; for a slave will either hate the one and love the other, or be devoted to the one and despise the other. You cannot serve God and wealth. (Matthew 6:24)

The word used here for wealth is *mammon*. Some translations, such as the NIV, capitalize this word to emphasise that Jesus is pitting one god against another. Both seek our allegiance and worship. Wealth is not neutral. It's insatiable—once you have some of it, you seem to keep wanting more and more of it. No wonder Jesus commented to his disciples after his encounter with the rich young man:

Truly I tell you, it will be hard for a rich person to enter the kingdom of heaven. Again I tell you, it is easier for a camel to go through the eye of a needle than for someone who is rich to enter the kingdom of God. (Matthew 19:23-24)

For Jesus then, wealth is a dangerous thing. It is like a stick of dynamite—having the potential to do much good, but also to cause a lot of damage. And the more you have, the greater the risks.

Fifthly, gaining provision and wealth may fuel dissatisfaction with what we have and, with it, the desire for more. Envy and covetousness can easily develop as we compare our lot with that of others who have more than we do. In fact, the drive to accumulate and to consume more makes us vulnerable to manipulation. As early as 1929, Floyd Allen, an executive with General Motors, put it bluntly—"Advertising is the business of making people helpfully dissatisfied with what they have in favor of something better."[8]

More recently, sociologist Bernard McGrane suggested that

One of the sub-texts of all advertising is, "You're not okay the way you are. Things are bad. You need help. You need salvation." In that sense, advertising is designed to generate endless self-criticism, all sorts of anxieties, and then to offer the entire world of consumer goods as your salvation…In contrast, one message you'll never hear in advertising is, "You're okay. You don't need anything. Just be yourself."[9]

We easily find ourselves perpetually desiring more. We have trained our appetites to always desire more. Working out what is enough is exceptionally challenging within this environment. Perhaps this is what James was addressing when he wrote:

You covet something and cannot obtain it; so you engage in disputes and conflicts. You do not have, because you do not ask. You ask and do not receive, because you ask wrongly, in order to spend what you get on your pleasures. (James 4:2-3)

Sixthly, we can become anxious and full of worry about the future provision of our needs. One would think that this kind of concern would only fill the hearts and minds of those who genuinely don't have enough. However, most people who have plenty also develop this insidious stress. Having more than the basic necessities seems to make us more anxious because now we have more stuff to worry about losing.

The fear of not having enough is what drives some people to work unnecessarily long hours under the pretext that to provide for their children means buying them the latest gadgets and fashionable clothes, when what they really need most is the parent's time and attention. Others are consumed by the fear that they won't have enough money to sustain them through their twilight years. And so they plan for their future provision at the cost of serving God and others in the here-and-now, developing rich and meaningful relationships, or living a balanced life.

Still others lie awake at night worrying about whether a particular investment is safe or dreaming of how to get the house or car they really want. In fact, more anxious energy is consumed on money matters than on almost anything else. Is it this anxiety that drives people to do things they normally wouldn't—like commit fraud, be less than honest, sacrifice a friendship or compromise their values?

Having more than the basic provision we need can be a burden. The well-known words of Jesus in Matthew 6—spoken to a crowd who knew what it was like to struggle to make ends meet—are particularly pertinent:

Do not worry, saying, "What will we eat?" or "What will we drink?" or "What will we wear?" For it is the Gentiles who strive for all these things; and indeed your heavenly Father knows that you need all these things. But strive first for the kingdom of God and his righteousness, and all these things will be given to you as well. (Matthew 6:31-33)

This is a very provocative statement of Jesus. It is not easy to trust God—particularly if your economic future is uncertain. However, as N.T. Wright notes: "When [Jesus] urged his followers not to worry about tomorrow, we must assume he led them by example."[10] If we ask, "Can anyone really trust God this way?" we can answer that at least one person did.

Redeeming the Economic Sphere

While it is true that God's original intention for humanity to enjoy his provision and wealth has been disrupted, the story is not finished. God's response to the lack of provision and wealth in the world is to redeem the economic sphere so that it again provides what everyone needs.

The Apostle Paul reminds us in Colossians that

In him all the fullness of God was pleased to dwell, and through him God was pleased to reconcile to himself *all* things, whether on earth or in heaven, by making peace through the blood of his cross. (Colossians 1:19-20)

"All things" includes the economic sphere.

A critical way God brings about this redemption is through the lives of Jesus' followers. Colossians continues,

You who were once estranged and hostile in mind, doing evil deeds, he has now reconciled in his fleshly body through death, so as to present you holy and blameless and irreproachable before him. (Colossians 1:21-22)

And in his second letter to the Corinthians, Paul expands on God's work in and through us:

If anyone is in Christ, there is a new creation; everything old has passed away, everything has become new! All this is from God, who reconciled us to himself through Christ, and has given us the ministry of reconciliation…entrusting the message of reconciliation to us. So we are ambassadors for Christ. (2 Corinthians 5:17-20)

This reconciliation with God has enormous implications for *every* aspect of our lives, including economics. Ambassadors, of course, represent their sovereigns' economic interests, along with all other interests.

So what might this mean for our role as Christ's ambassadors and redemptive partners?

We Are to Develop and Model Right Attitudes to Provision and Wealth

Redeeming our use of money resources begins with the nurturing of biblical attitudes—from which right actions will flow. Three fundamental biblical attitudes are trusteeship, gratitude and contentment.

From an Attitude of Ownership to Trusteeship

The first humans were directed by God to take care of the Garden and all creatures and plants within it. This is often called the "creation mandate." God shared the day-to-day management of the Garden with Adam and Eve. They were to view themselves as caretakers of the created order.

This trusteeship is built on the principle that ultimate ownership of everything we have and inhabit is not ours, but God's. God is the owner, who has entrusted management to us, to be exercised according to his purposes. As the Psalmist declares, "The earth is the Lord's and all that is in it" (Psalm 24:1). King David affirms the same in his prayer in front of the people of Israel, at the establishment of the Temple building fund. "All things come from you, and of your own have we given" (1 Chronicles 29:14b). We have no right to claim absolute ownership of any of our resources, neither money, possessions, business, abilities, physical environment nor heritage. We are merely trustees of whatever provision or wealth we receive.

Fiduciary duty, or stewardship, is a key element of trusteeship. While trustees are given a great deal of freedom to act and make decisions regarding resource allocation, they do so *on behalf* of the true owners or beneficiaries of the body they manage. And, of course, the greater the resources entrusted to them, the greater their responsibility. Jesus picks up on this in his parable of the faithful or unfaithful slave, noting that, "From everyone to whom much has been given, much will be required; and from the one to whom much has been entrusted, even more will be demanded" (Luke 12:48b). Craig Blomberg puts it this way: "People in positions of power have no increased privilege—just increased responsibility!"[11]

Acting as trustees of whatever wealth we have been given, is therefore foundational to a biblical perspective on provision and wealth. These resources are not for us to do with as we please. How we use them is not our business alone either. While God does not expect us to live on nothing, he does require us to maximise our resources for the building of God's kingdom. Those fortunate enough to be born into affluence have a responsibility to use their wealth to provide for those who don't have enough. They may accomplish this in a variety of ways, including donations, investments, and direct service.

The command to use our resources for the benefit of poor people is given directly in the book of Exodus.

For six years you shall sow your land and gather in its yield; but the seventh year you shall let it rest and lie fallow, so that the poor of your people may eat; and what they leave the wild animals may eat. You shall do the same with your vineyard, and with your olive orchard. (Exodus 23:10–11)

Whoever owns land has a duty to let the poor use it free of charge one year in every seven, and even to let wild animals make use of it. This command is repeated in Deuteronomy in even simpler terms:

Since there will never cease to be some in need on the earth, I therefore command you, "Open your hand to the poor and needy neighbor in your land." (Deuteronomy 15:11)

The crucial point is that we are not to hoard the resources entrusted to us for ourselves, maintaining lifestyles, homes and church facilities beyond what is needed.

Trusteeship reminds us *who* we are working for—God—and for *what* we are working toward—God's kingdom. It centres us in a new economy and a different dream, one framed by God's agenda for this world, and for us. As partners with God we have been called to participate in this cause with all the resources at our disposal—including our wealth.

From an Attitude of Ingratitude to Gratitude

If we understand that everything we have is God's—including the very capacity to work, engage in business, create and produce, sell, and build wealth—we will be grateful to God.

Of course, if we are wealthy and have abundance, it's easy to convince ourselves that what we have is mainly a result of our own hard work, intelligence and creative genius. The reality is quite the opposite. If we have been born into a loving family, a prosperous country, a good educational system, a stable society with the rule of law, we have the good fortune needed to make it possible for hard work to pay off. This is not to suggest that hard work never contributes to economic success. Clearly, it is often a factor. Yet even intelligence and creative genius needed to make hard work fruitful are gifts from God. The Apostle Paul puts it bluntly when he asks the Corinthians, "What do you have that you did not receive? And if you received it, why do you boast as if it were not a gift?" (1 Corinthians 4:7). Paul's point is that even the very abilities we have are given to us by God. King David echoes this sentiment when in response to God's generosity he prays, "Who am I, O Lord God, and what is my house, that you have brought me thus far?" (1 Chronicles 17:16). Biblically, the response to the blessing of provision and abundance is deep gratitude, even if our own work played a major role in generating our wealth.

Yet even among Christians, affluence seems to breed ingratitude and a sense of entitlement—as if we are somehow owed something. This betrays an inflated view of our own importance, and a very limited awareness of gift, grace and good fortune in our lives. Another factor that prevents us from experiencing gratitude is envy. It is easy to begrudge others for what *they* have, rather than being content and grateful for what *we* have if we see ourselves primarily as consumers, rather than servants. Western culture feeds this envy. Marketing, advertising, and even entertainment encourage us to make living like the rich our aspiration. In doing so, we crave for what others have—not only their possessions but also their abilities and circumstances. In contrast, the Bible commands us not to covet anything that belongs to our neighbor—whether positions at work, salaries, economic opportunities or bank balances—but to develop a growing gratitude for what *we* have been given.

How can we become more thankful? By giving thanks. We become more thankful through the simple act of giving thanks every day for whatever we have that we appreciate. Giving thanks actually changes our attitude. If, at the same time, we turn off or tune out the "aspirational" marketing and cultural messages, we can actually become more thankful and joyful in our lives.

From an Attitude of Discontentment to Contentment

Gratitude leads to contentment. Contentment is a delicious feeling in itself, and it is the antidote to greed and envy. The Bible presents a vision for economic life that doesn't depend on ever-increasing consumption to prevent us from feeling disappointed. In this vision, it is possible to have enough and to cease longing for more. The Israelites experienced this in the wilderness, when every day God gave them exactly enough bread ("manna") from heaven. "Those who gathered much had nothing over, and those who gathered little had no shortage; they gathered as much as each of them needed" (Exodus 16:18). Hebrews counsels us, "Keep your lives free from the love of money, and be *content* with what you have" (Hebrews 13:5). In the same vein, Paul writes, "Of course, there is great gain in godliness combined with contentment; for we brought nothing into the world, so that we can take nothing out of it; but if we have food and clothing, we will be content with these" (1 Timothy 6:6-8). And in a letter written from a prison cell, Paul shares something of his own journey.

Not that I am referring to being in need; for I have learned to be content with whatever I have. I know what it is to have little, and I know what it is to have plenty. In any and all circumstances I have learned the secret of being well-fed and of going hungry, of having plenty and of being in need. I can do all things through him who strengthens me. (Philippians 4:11-13)

Both Paul and the far-from-wealthy Philippian church he is writing to were barely surviving economically. Their attitude of being content in all economic situations challenges those who live in plenty to find contentment in what they have.

Contentment is knowing what is enough. What is enough profit? Pay? Hours employed? Savings accumulated? House size? Possessions? Given that none of us have a true gauge on what is sufficient and what is excessive, we will need help from others. What would it be like for Christians to meet in small groups to share their purchasing plans and reflect together whether they reflect true needs leading to gratitude and contentment, or envious aspirations that will lead merely to a sense of entitlement and discontent? So few Christians have tried this that it is hard to know what effect it might have simply to share our ideas about what is enough in practical terms.

We Are to Change Our Personal Lifestyles

Developing right attitudes to provision and wealth will inevitably lead to adjustment in the way we live.

From a Lifestyle of Self-Sufficient Individualism to Community

One of the more frequent words translated as "community" or "fellowship" in the New Testament is *koinonia*. This was a well-used word in the Greek world. In ordinary usage, it referred to having something in common with someone. However, the Bible's use of *koinonia* emphasizes active participation—owning a share in something, rather than just being associated with it. When Paul, in particular, uses *koinonia*, it carries this strong sense of partnership, including the call to financial partnership.[12] A prime example of this is Paul's commendation of the Corinthians for the "generosity of your sharing [*koinonias*]," (2 Corinthians 9:13) referring to the money they donated for the relief of poor Christians in Jerusalem. Another example is the distribution of resources among the first "fellowship" (*koinonia*, Acts 2:42) of Christians. This fellowship was both spiritual and financial, with the result that "there was not a needy person among them" (Acts 4:32-35). God provided for the needs of the individuals, through the resources of community. "All who believed were together and had all things in common; they would sell their possessions and goods and distribute the proceeds to all, as any had need" (Acts 2:44–45).

Although there is little indication that communal holding of wealth occurred outside this brief period in the New Testament church, it is clear the community in Jerusalem tried to realize God's vision that provision and wealth are communal, not individual, matters. Of course, how this might be expressed in our various twenty-first century contexts will depend on a variety of factors. History has shown that collective ownership generally works out poorly. Yet some still practice full economic sharing within a highly-trusted community. Other faith communities might seek to pool donations from the wealthy to distribute to the poor. Still others might choose to give individually to specific people or to charitable organizations that provide for needy people. The Bible prescribes not the method, but the attitude. God provides for his people in the plural, even though the resources may be entrusted to individuals as stewards.

From a Lifestyle of Isolationism to Personal Engagement

The temptation of those who have much to become isolated from those who have little is very real. High-fenced houses, air-conditioned cars, a circle of friends limited to our own socio-economic group, and a church similarly restricted—all these conspire to keep the well-to-do trapped in their own wealthy enclaves. Those who have little are effectively banished from their world.

This means wealthy people often have minimal or no relationship with those who struggle financially—either at home or abroad. Their understanding of the circumstances of those who lack basic provision is severely limited by the geographic and social distance.

As noted earlier, the people of Israel were specifically commanded to care for widows, orphans (fatherless) and foreigners.[13] In an agrarian society these groups were particularly vulnerable because they had no access to land or means of income. These same factors made them prone to isolation. To care for them, the people of Israel would first have to engage with them personally. God himself is described by the Psalms as relating personally to them as the "father of orphans and protector of widows" (Psalm 68:5).

This same hospitality—the welcoming of "strangers"—is fundamental to following Jesus. Two key gospel passages—Luke 14:12-14 (inviting the poor to your banquet) and Matthew 25:31-46 (God's judgment of the peoples)—shape the distinction between conventional and Christian hospitality. Conventional hospitality is shown to friends and family. Christian hospitality extends to the poor and "the least of these" (Matthew 25:40), the people who "cannot repay you" (Luke 14:14) or "invite you in return" (Luke 14:12). Jesus emphasizes the dimension of personal relationship in this case, when he states, "Truly I tell you, just as you did it to one of the least of these who are members of my family, *you did it to me*" (Matthew 25:40). Though the context indicates that Jesus is referring primarily to his disciples ("members of my family") there is no reason to suggest that disciples should not also take the same attitude to those who are not Christians. After all, Christ died for us "while we were still sinners" and before we ourselves were members of his family.

When those who have much get to know those who have little, perspectives can change. Hearing their stories, seeing their struggles first-hand, realizing that there is much to learn from them and also that we all have much in common—these all reshape our minds and hearts. God himself took on human flesh to draw close to us personally as a human (Philippians 2:6-8), and because of this he is able to "sympathize with our weaknesses" (Hebrews 4:15). If God thinks it worthwhile to encounter we who are poor and weak compared to him, should we not follow his example and encounter those who are poor and weak compared to us? The poor are no longer just faceless numbers. They become real people with real needs and real lives.

It is important for Christians to think generously about *how* such hospitality is given. While giving and investing money are essential means of expressing hospitality, more personal and closer-to-home expressions are also important. Within every community there are many types of strangers, as we have seen. The problem is that for many people in well-paying jobs, living in well-to-do neighbourhoods, mixing in affluent friendship groups, and worshipping in prosperous church congregations, connecting with the poor is not likely to be a part of everyday life. Building personal relationships will require intentionally moving out of accustomed circles and into uncomfortable situations. It may even require geographic travel or relocation. And if it is to be genuine Christian hospitality, as such it will need to avoid paternalism (which disempowers others by doing for them what they can do for themselves) and seek to minimize power imbalances. This may particularly be a challenge for those who experience financial success, and for whom status and success are the predominant currencies of self-worth. It is hard to shed the prestige and privileges of power when our instinct is to fix problems from afar rather than to encounter people in the midst of their struggles.

One of the biblical characters who models this kind of personal engagement with the poor is Job. Job's life intersected with the poor of his district on a regular basis. He was not isolated from them but lived in close proximity to his servants, widows, the fatherless and the stranger/foreigner.

The stranger has not lodged in the street; I have opened my doors to the traveler. (Job 31:32)

I delivered the poor who cried, and the orphan who had no helper…I caused the widow's heart to sing for joy…I was eyes to the blind, and feet to the lame. I was a father to the needy, and I championed the cause of the stranger. (Job 29:12-13, 15-16)

Job knew his poor neighbors, treated them as equals, felt a deep compassion for them and cared for them using his political and financial resources.

From a Lifestyle of Compulsive Work to a Rhythm of Work and Rest

Back to Table of Contents

Learning to trust God for our provision is an ongoing challenge, particularly if we are prone to compulsive work habits. Gordon MacDonald, a U.S. pastor, observes of his culture:

The more we want, the more revenue we must produce to get it. The more revenue we must produce, the longer and harder we have to work. So we build larger homes, buy more cars, take on added financial burdens and then find ourselves having to work harder to pay for it all. More work, less rest.[14]

But compulsive work habits are not limited to those who struggle with affluent culture. They are also the temptation of those who struggle to simply provide the basic necessities for themselves and their families.

Either way, the biblical practice of Sabbath is important for maintaining a Godly perspective on provision and wealth. For the people of Israel, the weekly Sabbath (ceasing from work) was part of their covenantal responsibility—a day to re-centre on God, and to celebrate his love for them. It was a gift from God to keep his people liberated from the grinding toil described in Genesis 3. It was a kindness, an example of God's care.

The Sabbath rest is a regular repudiation of the covetousness for more. It is a statement to ourselves that there are other things in life besides producing and consuming. And that there is more to our identity than what we do or what we produce. We are not the sum total of our bank accounts, nor of the work or responsibilities we carry.

The Sabbath rest comes down to an act of trust. To observe it, we must dare to trust God to provide for our needs, rather than working all-out to provide for them ourselves. This is a hard lesson to learn, and it usually takes trial and error for us to really get it, as Israel discovered when depending on God's provision of manna in the desert (Exodus 16:1-36). And it is a reminder that ultimately life depends not on our hard graft, but on God's provision and grace. This is a challenge—both for those who struggle with the prospect of not having enough and for those who struggle with the peril of not recognizing what is enough.

See our article *Balancing Rhythms of Rest and Work: Overview* for an in-depth discussion of this topic.

We Are to Use Our Wealth for the Aid of Those in Poverty

Developing right attitudes to provision and wealth and making changes in our personal lives are a starting point for partnering with God to redeem the economic sphere of life. However, there is also a strong and consistent mandate throughout Scripture for those with wealth to use it to aid those in poverty. The most obvious way (and the one most written about in the Bible) is through giving. However, investing and judicious spending are also valid responses to helping the poor.

Aiding the Poor Through Giving

When we are genuinely aware of the presence of God's grace in our lives, our grateful hearts inevitably overflow into generous giving. Jesus directs his disciples, "Freely you have received, freely give" (Matthew 10:8). This is exactly what happened to the churches in Macedonia, as described in 2 Corinthians, chapters 8 and 9. These chapters form the fullest articulation in the New Testament of the practice of generosity and giving. According to Paul, the Macedonian churches spontaneously gave to the church in Jerusalem for the relief of its members enduring economic distress. Yet the Macedonian Christians themselves were poor. Paul tells us that

During a severe ordeal of affliction, their abundant joy and their extreme poverty have overflowed in a wealth of generosity on their part. For, as I can testify, they voluntarily gave according to their means, and even beyond their means, begging us earnestly for the privilege of sharing in this ministry to the saints." (2 Corinthians 8:2-4)

What is striking is that they did not give out of abundance, but in the midst of their own struggles. If we are ever to become givers, we have to begin giving now, out of whatever little we think we have. If we wait until we think we have enough, we will never have enough.

Paul observes that Jesus himself is the model for such giving. "For you know the generous act of our Lord Jesus Christ, that though he was rich, yet for your sakes he became poor, so that by his poverty you might become rich" (2 Corinthians 8:9). Why are we to give? It is because the One whom we follow modeled generosity to us.

Paul goes on to argue that the wealthy should give to such an extent—and the poor should receive to such an extent—that a fair distribution results.

I do not mean that there should be relief for others and pressure on you, but it is a question of a fair balance between your present abundance and their need, so that their abundance may be for your need, in order that there may be a fair balance. As it is written, "The one who had much did not have too much, and the one who had little did not have too little." (2 Corinthians 8:13–15)

His line of thought suggests that there are extremes of both wealth and poverty that are out of place in the Christian community. If there are brothers and sisters who are unable to provide for their basic needs, those who have a surplus need to respond. This is immensely challenging to most Christians in the West, whose wealth far exceeds that of Christians in most of the world who struggle to survive on a day-to-day basis.

Yet Paul does not aim to use guilt to motivate us. Our giving should be characterized not just by generosity, but also by joy. "Each of you must give as you have made up your mind, not reluctantly or under compulsion, for God loves a cheerful giver" (2 Corinthians 9:7). We should give because we want to, willingly—out of the overflow of a thankful heart. If we don't want to give, let us pay more attention to the practice of thankfulness and see if that will give us a cheerful heart for giving.

It is not easy to give generously. It is personally counterintuitive and deeply counter-cultural. On a personal level we fear that if we give generously, we won't have enough for our own needs. Our culture reinforces this fear by presenting ever-increasing "needs" to us, and by appealing to our desire to find security by owning and hoarding. Only by the power of God's spirit can we hope to break free of the grip of wealth enough to give generously. Yet if we receive the gift of generosity from God, it is the gift of liberty from personal enslavement to wealth and cultural enslavement to the false gods of security and status.

Of course, having determined to give, the questions of *where* and *how* need to be answered. Wisdom is required to discern the most helpful and appropriate of a myriad of options. When choosing to give through an agency, two considerations might be:

- Does this organization empower the people they are seeking to assist? Do they listen well and work with the recipients to tailor assistance to what is most helpful? Do they pay attention to the cultural context in which they work? Or are they so intent on doing what they think is needed in the way they think is right that they inadvertently make matters worse?
- Is the organization transparent and honest regarding how they use their resources and how effective they are? Are they accountable to an independent board of directors and do they submit financial reports to international monitoring organizations? Sadly, it is not uncommon for organisations to lack integrity by exaggerating their claims, being less than open to independent audit or evaluation, prone to wasting resources, or spending unnecessary funds on administration, fundraising, high salaries for executives, etc.

Aiding the Poor Through Investing

While giving is a fundamental way of using wealth to aid those caught in poverty, wise investment of wealth can also be very effective in helping the poor. There are many examples of how this can be achieved. However, over recent decades two broad movements illustrate what can be achieved by investment in the poorest communities.

The first is the world of microfinance. Across the globe, though particularly in developing nations, co-operatives are established in poor communities to make loans to initiate small businesses. As these businesses generate income, the start-up loan is paid back and the capital lent to new small businesses. At least, this is the intention. The effectiveness of microfinance seems to be uneven in various contexts, and it has its share of supporters and of critics. However, at its best, it is a mechanism for those with entrepreneurial abilities to obtain capital, create a value-adding business, provide for themselves, and benefit their communities.

A second broad form of microfinance is that of "savings-led" co-operatives, which rather than giving loans to members, asks them to commit to saving a small amount each week, which is then aggregated with the rest of the group and eventually invested. Over time, with support and mentoring, the co-operative builds a reservoir of capital, which can be drawn on by individuals for urgent needs or borrowed in order to begin a business. The shared capital can also be used for enhancing the well-being of the whole community. Savings-led co-operatives help poor communities to overcome one of the primary barriers for people improving their lot—that is, a lack of options for safely investing their minuscule savings.

Another movement growing in both developed and developing nations is that of "social enterprise." These are businesses that are established to achieve social goals in addition to being profitable. Such enterprises often seek to generate a "sustainable" profit, but not necessarily to maximize return on investment.

A few examples of such enterprises are:[15]

- **Sarah and John** have set up a pottery business and only employ people who have multiple barriers to finding work. Workers may be homeless or semi-homeless and may have mental health issues, physical disabilities, substance addictions or other struggles. The employment is not full-time, but it does provide a supplement to whatever other means of support workers receive. The pottery is sold through specialty shops and also through the Internet.
- **Michael** runs a business assembling and exporting electronic components. He employs people with autism spectrum disorder (also known as Asperger's syndrome), training them to do the highly delicate work. The business is only small (employing up to 12 workers at any one time), but the opportunity to train, mentor and develop people who otherwise would struggle to get work, is central to his motivation and decision-making.
- **XYZ organization** has established a jute bag making business in the red light district of a major Asian city. Bags are exported all over the world and are known for their durability and quality. The business only employs women who have been caught up in prostitution or are vulnerable to it. Offering women a way out of the entrapment of selling their bodies in order to feed their families, the jute bag factory provides meaningful alternative employment at a livable wage, plus the benefit of a supportive community.

- **Jerry** has operated an importing business for some years. Though he doesn't employ anyone, he has invested considerable resources in order to build a business that is sustainable and profitable. He pays himself a livable wage and all profits are given away to a microfinance project in the developing world.

Although we have focused on investment vehicles that explicitly seek to aid poor people, ordinary for-profit business investments in poor countries and communities can also be powerful means of reducing poverty. The productive capacity of the world is not close to being exhausted, although human ingenuity and diligent stewardship of natural resources and the environment are required.

However, because the purpose of businesses is generally to benefit shareholders, not poor communities, they can also become powerful means of exploitation and abuse. Hundreds of millions of Christians work in businesses that invest in, manufacture, distribute, sell or transport goods and services in poor regions. Perhaps they have the greatest opportunity of all to shape business strategy and operations in ways that aid poor people throughout the world.

Poor people and spending

It may seem odd to suggest that spending is potentially a way to aid those in poverty. We often associate spending with excessive consumption. Many Christians hold a frugality mentality that regards spending as vaguely ungodly. This may be true if spending means not buying things we don't need. But it often comes out instead as a desire to buy things cheaply, whether we need them or not. Somehow getting a bargain assuages our misgivings about buying things. But the result may be that we contribute to the pricing pressures that lead manufacturers to pay workers too little to support themselves and their families.

In some cases, spending *more* for the items we consume may improve the lives of those who make and sell them. In the present global economy, many workers are paid too little to provide for their daily needs. Meanwhile, those who purchase the goods and services they provide could easily afford to pay a higher price for the items. If there were a way for consumers to pay more—and for that increase to go to the workers who need it—spending could actually help aid poor people.

Over the past few decades, a whole movement has grown in the developed world to seek to pay fair prices for products made in the developing world. "Fair trade" looks to compensate small coffee, cocoa, cotton growers, craft makers, and other small industries, equitably for their work.

Spending money is also commended in the Bible when the money is spent in generosity to others. God commends spending lavishly on a dinner party for your neighbours, provided you are not looking for anything in return (Luke 14:12-14). It is only lavish spending *on your own pleasures* that the Bible forbids (James 4:3). So if our question is, "what should I do with the money I have?" then "spend lavishly on wonderful things for others when you expect nothing in return," would be a good answer. However, this moves beyond the present topic of spending *to aid the poor*, so we will end this discussion here.

We Are to Change the Organizations and Structures of Society

Christians are called to work not only at the small enterprise and person-to-person level in seeking to alleviate poverty, but also at the macro or structural level. The world contains resources enough to meet everyone's needs. But the social, political and economic motivation and means to do so have never come together on a global scale. This too is a form of human sin and error. We are to be involved in changing the organizations and systems of provision and wealth in our societies. Although we may feel too small and insignificant, too far removed from the halls of power in our society, God has a habit of using outsiders and insignificant people to bring great economic changes in societies.

Perhaps the first agent of structural change in a foreign land was Joseph (Genesis 41-42). Born in the insignificant land of Canaan, sold into slavery in Egypt, imprisoned on false charges, and otherwise marginalized, he eventually reformed the economic structures of the great nation of Egypt. With great prophetic foresight, he implemented an extensive network of storage cities, where harvested grain from the good productive years could be kept for times of famine. These were the original food banks! As a result, the capacity of the Egyptians to provide sufficiently for their people during the long years of famine, was masterfully increased and there was ample to feed everyone—even enough to provide for Joseph's estranged family who ventured south in search of food. Without Joseph's willingness to challenge the economic systems of Egypt, millions of poor people would have died during the seven years of famine that struck. But because he did challenge and change the system, poor and rich alike were able to survive.

Likewise, when the nation of Israel was held captive in Babylon, they found themselves powerless and disenfranchised. Yet the prophet Jeremiah counselled God's people to "seek the peace and prosperity of the city and pray to the Lord on its behalf, for in its welfare you will find your welfare" (Jeremiah 29:7). God's purposes were for his people to reform the structures of their own captors.

This became possible when a few young men, Daniel, Shadrach, Meshach and Abednego, were drafted into leadership roles within the Babylonian government. Rather than succumbing to the temptations of luxury afforded by their new positions, they challenged the system. They risked their positions—and their lives—to fight injustice and inequity. By acting as agents of change, Daniel and his friends worked for—not against—the prosperity of their host nation. God's intention was to use them to redeem the system, culture and society where they lived and worked. In one case, this meant Daniel challenging the king directly. "O king, may my counsel be acceptable to you: atone for your sins with righteousness, and your inequities with mercy to the oppressed, so that your prosperity may be prolonged" (Daniel 4:27).

Wherever we find ourselves working—in government departments, political parties, non-governmental organizations, municipal structures, multinational corporations, small businesses, health or education systems, local neighborhoods—we too should seek to work for the welfare and prosperity of those we serve. At times this will mean challenging systems and structures that stand in the way of God's provision and prosperity for all people. This may require changing the priorities, structures, and processes of such organizations—particularly where they oppress or marginalize the vulnerable or the poor. Whether it be in advocating for fairer taxation systems, helping draft legislation against monopolistic or anti-competitive practices, or challenging the way employers and unions relate to each other in a particular industry, there are many opportunities for Christians to bring systemic change to the way provision and wealth are obtained.

CONTENT NOT YET AVAILABLE: The closely-related topic of economic systems is discussed in depth in the article **Economics and Society* at www.theologyofwork.org.

We Are to Work With Non-Believers to Increase Provision and Reduce Poverty

At a number of points in Scripture, God uses those who aren't his followers, to bring about his purposes. One example, in the Book of Ezra, concerns Cyrus the Persian.

In the first year of King Cyrus of Persia, in order that the word of the Lord by the mouth of Jeremiah might be accomplished, the Lord stirred up the spirit of King Cyrus of Persia so that he sent a herald throughout all his kingdom, and also in a written edict declared: "Thus says King Cyrus of Persia: The Lord, the God of heaven, has given me all the kingdoms of the earth, and he has charged me to build him a house at Jerusalem in Judah…" (Ezra 1:1-2)

Remarkably, God chooses to appoint someone not of God's people to do the work of the Lord. God is not restricted to bringing about his redemptive purposes by working solely through his own people. Like Ezra (and later in the story, Nehemiah) we also can work with non-believers to redeem the world.

One way of doing this is partnering with individuals and organizations who are seeking to improve the economic realities of the poor in all kinds of ways. There are many non-Christian individuals and institutions undertaking great work in providing meaningful employment, small business opportunities, poverty relief and community development. We can work in solidarity and partnership with such people and causes. Of course, we need to be discerning here. It is important to ensure that the effects of such partnerships are consistent with biblical aims and values.

Nehemiah - A Positive Role Model

Nehemiah is one biblical character whose attitudes, lifestyle, strategies and priorities work together to change society for the betterment of poor people. As governor of the city of Jerusalem—working for a foreign power—he risks his position to advocate rebuilding of the city walls in order to protect the native (mostly poor) Jewish population. Nehemiah is well rewarded materially for his leadership role. It would have been easy for him just to enjoy the privileges that went with his position. Yet when Nehemiah is approached by a group of Jews who are struggling economically, he intervenes to help them. Like many Jews, they had ended up with crippling debt, forfeited their land, even becoming enslaved, because many wealthy people exploited unfair advantages during a tough economic climate. Nehemiah's response is to publicly denounce the exploiters and challenge them to give back what they had taken. Remarkably they did! Additionally, Nehemiah organizes a relief program for those in distress and institutes long-term financial reforms to ensure those impoverished were able to develop a livelihood again.

But the most remarkable feature of Nehemiah's response is a costly, personal change of lifestyle. Having observed how his predecessors and their assistants "laid heavy burdens on the people" and lorded it over them, Nehemiah chooses to reduce his income, live more simply and refuse many of the benefits he was entitled to. To reduce the tax burden on the people, he takes over the expense of 150 Jews, officials and foreigners, serving in his administration. In doing so he expresses a generous hospitality, hosting them daily at his own table (Nehemiah 5:14-19). See "Restoration of the Wall of Jerusalem (Nehemiah 1:1-7:73)" in "Ezra, Nehemiah & Esther and Work" at www.theologyofwork.org for more about Nehemiah's use of his wealth for the good of the people of Israel.

Hope and Help in God's Provision

What then, is reasonable to expect from God in regard to provision for our own needs?

We Can Seek Guidance About Provision from God...

We can seek guidance about provision from God and expect that doing so will help us meet our needs, the needs of those who depend on us, and the needs of the world. Jesus states,

Ask, and it will be given you...For everyone who asks receives...Is there anyone among you who, if your child asks for bread, will give a stone? Or if the child asks for a fish, will give a snake? If you then, who are evil, know how to give good gifts to your children, how much more will your Father in heaven give good things to those who ask him! (Matthew 7:7-11)

After acknowledging and thanking the church at Philippi for their gift to him while he languished in house arrest in Rome, Paul confidently states, "My God will fully satisfy every need of yours according to his riches in glory in Christ Jesus" (Philippians 4:19).

Does this mean that if we don't have enough to provide for our needs and the needs of those around us, we should ask God for help? Yes. We do not have God's promise that he will provide everything we desire immediately. But we do have his promise to give us what we need. We should ask for his guidance in practical ways if we are in need. We can ask his guidance in finding a job, applying for benefits, changing jobs, resolving employee-employer disputes, obtaining education and job training. We should ask for his transforming power in our workplace ethics, creativity and productivity, work habits and other factors needed to keep a job and thrive in the workplace. If we are unemployed or under-employed, our disappointment or shame may lead us to back away from God. But these are the moments to draw closer to God more than ever.

Looking to God for help doesn't just apply to those who lack provision. If we have wealth, the choices in how to earn, invest and give are often bewilderingly complex. In such situations, we need God's guidance and direction in deciding how to gain and use such resources well—in ways that honour God and don't harm ourselves or others. James instructs, "If any of you is lacking in wisdom, ask God, who gives to all generously and ungrudgingly, and it will be given to you" (James 1:5).

We Are Meant to Depend on God for Provision…

We are meant to depend on God for provision, meaning that we should look to him to provide for us when our own means seem inadequate.

The miracle of Jesus feeding five thousand people is the premier biblical example of God providing when our own means seem inadequate. A large crowd follows Jesus as he goes into a remote area. They become hungry, and there is no place to buy food and no money to buy it with, anyway. One of the disciples discovers a boy who has a mere five barley loaves and two fish. Jesus receives these meagre supplies, gives thanks, and has them distributed to the whole crowd, as if they were a meal for thousands. Astonishingly, everyone in the crowd is able to take as much as they wanted. "When they were satisfied, he told his disciples, 'Gather up the fragments left over, so that nothing may be lost'" (John 6:11-12). And when they do, they fill twelve baskets! (John 6:1-14; see also Matthew 14:13-21, Mark 6:30-44, and Luke 9:10-17).

God delights in making up what we lack. This is a reminder that none of us are self-sufficient. God *is* our provider.

We Are Meant to Work Diligently and Wisely…

We are meant to work diligently and wisely to the degree we are able. Dependence on God is an attitude towards human labour, not a substitute for it.

Although God is our provider, he calls us to use what we have in our hands, not what we haven't. God's first gift to us for our provision is our ability to work, as we have seen in Genesis 1 and 2. Our work does not stand on its own, as a substitute for God's generosity, but it is generally the first ingredient in God's provision. Even if disability, circumstances or injustice make our work fall tragically short of meeting our needs, God begins by making use of what we *are* able to do. Then he makes up the difference from his inexhaustible riches.

In response to news that there were some in the church in Thessalonica who were shirking work, Paul commands,

Anyone unwilling to work should not eat. For we hear that some of you are living in idleness, mere busybodies, not doing any work. Now such persons we command and exhort in the Lord Jesus Christ to do their work quietly and to earn their own living (2 Thessalonians 3:10-12).

No work, no eat. This, of course, presumes that there is work to do. It does not matter whether that work is paid or not. If there is useful work we can do, we cannot sit idle and expect God to bless our idleness. Many households depend on paid work done outside the household and unpaid work done within. Both kinds of work are elements of God's provision. Even those who need paid work, but who are unemployed or unable to hold down a paid job, can still work in voluntary capacities. It is our responsibility to work to the degree we are able, even if it is God's job to ensure that our needs are met. Idleness is not a valid form of dependence on God.

God Does Not Promise That Christians Will Escape the Effects of the Fallen World

Nowhere in Scripture does God promise that his followers will escape the effects of the fallen world. In fact, most of the biblical characters endured periods of time where circumstances, suffering and persecution robbed them of what they needed materially.

- **Joseph** spent years languishing in an Egyptian jail cell, no doubt with minimal rations to keep him healthy.
- **Naomi** felt the pain of living on the edge of survival—with no husband or land to provide for her and her daughter-in-law, Ruth.
- **Paul** endured harrowing experiences, including "toil and hardship, through many a sleepless night, hungry and thirsty, often without food, cold and naked" (2 Corinthians 11:27).

God does not exempt us from the sufferings of the world, but he protects us from being overcome by them. Jesus prayed to the Father on behalf of his disciples, "I am not asking you to take them out of the world, but I ask you to protect them from the evil one" (John 17:15).

Encouragement to Cultivate Generosity, in Good Seasons and Bad (Click to Listen)

So what does God promise? Provision for our needs, not our wants. Help to endure and overcome whatever deprivations, sufferings and trials we experience. And, most of all, that God will use all situations we find ourselves in—including when we lack provision—to bring good. For himself, for us, and for the world. As the most well-known of verses in Romans states, "We know that all things work together for good for those who love God, who are called according to his purpose" (Romans 8:28).

Wealth is No Indication of God's Favour or Blessing

Some churches preach what may be called a "health and wealth gospel," claiming that God always rewards his people with prosperity in this world. But in the Bible, wealth is no indication of God's favor. Neither is poverty an indication of God's punishment. "[God] makes his sun rise on the evil and on the good, and sends rain on the righteous and on the unrighteous" (Matthew 5:45).

Advocates of the health-and-wealth gospel often note that in the Old Testament, many of the characters we most revere were wealthy. They include Abraham, Isaac, Jacob, Joseph, Boaz, Job, David and Solomon. And there is little doubt that their experience of abundance was tied in some way to their faithfulness to God. Biblical scholar Craig Blomberg notes that in the Old Testament,

Wealth *can* be a sign of God's blessing, even if it is not always related to an individual's or a nation's obedience. But the unique covenantal arrangements between God and Israel prevent us from generalizing and saying that God must materially reward his faithful people in other nations or eras.[16]

Therefore, a strong connection between righteousness and wealth is difficult to make. The story of the people of Israel confirms this assessment. Many wealthy people in the Bible prosper because of their wickedness, not righteousness. These include a number of King David's descendants. For example, in 1 Kings 21 we read that King Ahab lusted after Naboth's land and when he failed to acquire it by fair means, his wife Jezebel had Naboth executed. This, even though Ahab was already unbelievably wealthy.

The association between righteousness and wealth is even more tenuous in the New Testament. In fact, biblical scholar Gordon Fee argues that wealth is *never* related to a life of obedience in the gospels and other New Testament books.[17] While we find a handful of well-to-do believers such as Joseph of Arimathea and Lydia, there is no suggestion by any of the New Testament writers that God's favor is particularly on those who have wealth. In fact, if anything the opposite is true.

For example, following his encounter with the rich young ruler, Jesus comments that it is easier for a rich man to pass through the eye of a needle than enter the kingdom. The shock of this statement causes his disciples to ask, "Then who can be saved?" (Matthew 19:25). In other words, "If not a rich man, then surely there's no hope for anyone else?" In a culture where wealth was presumed to be an indication of God's favour and blessing, Jesus' assertion was unequivocal. Wealth is not a sign of righteousness or God's favour. Instead, it is a grave peril to our relationship with God.

The Final Hope

The final hope of Christians is not to be spared the suffering that all people experience in the fallen world. It is to participate in the abundant life promised when the world is fully redeemed upon Christ's return. In the new earth there will be plenty for all. No one will lack provision. Justice will reign. Wealth will be experienced by all, without harm to anyone or anything. We will not suffer a lack of provision ourselves. We will not enrich ourselves at others' expense. All will be as God always intended it to be.

Isaiah prophesies about that time:

I am about to create new heavens and a new earth; the former things shall not be remembered or come to mind.... They shall build houses and inhabit them; they shall plant vineyards and eat their fruit. They shall not build and another inhabit; they shall not plant and another eat...They shall not labour in vain, or bear children for calamity. I will extend prosperity to her [Jerusalem] like a river, and the wealth of nations like an overflowing stream. (Isaiah 65:17, 21-23; 66:12)

John too foretells the prosperity of the New Jerusalem. God's provision is so extravagant that the gates of the city will be pearls, the foundations jewels, and the streets gold (Revelation

21:19-21). If the vision sounds a bit fantastical, perhaps it means that God's generosity is literally unimaginable to us, accustomed as we are to scarcity.

What then can we say in conclusion about provision and wealth in the Bible?

If we are wealthy, we are to be grateful and thankful for the blessing of wealth and seek God's guidance how to handle this wealth without harming ourselves, others or the environment. We are to learn to be content with what we have and as God's trustees, put our wealth at his disposal through acts of giving, wise investment and responsible spending. Recognizing the dangers of riches, we should ask for God's grace to not become proud, corrupt, self-sufficient, exploitative or complacent. And perhaps most of all, we are not to imagine that we are especially favoured by God.

If we are poor or struggling to provide enough for our needs we are to ask God for guidance and help. Resisting the urge to be overcome by anxiety or despair, we can look for God's grace to remain generous and joyful, even finding a way to be more content with less than we desire. Most of all, we should ask God for his grace not to imagine we are less valuable to God or are being punished by him.

If we feel we are neither rich nor poor just getting by, as it seems we are to express gratitude for what we *have* received and ask for God's guidance how to use it well. Being on the guard for worry, we should rejoice in the opportunity our economic situation provides to trust God daily for our needs. We are called to learn contentment and practice generosity beyond what we feel we can afford. Even when we feel uncertain of our own security, we are called to work for economic justice, though it might seem to threaten our own prospects. Together the practices of thankfulness, contentment, generosity and justice may show us more clearly the difference between what we feel we need and what is truly best for us. Perhaps they will prepare us to trust God's promises to provide for us.

Rich, poor or somewhere in-between, we can look forward in confidence to a future where there is no more struggle and none will lack anything. We will live in abundance in the renewed earth. God's vision for us and for his world will be fulfilled.

Anxiety about Money (Devotional)

Devotional

If you worry about money but feel powerless against anxiety, this plan is for you.

Provision (Genesis 1:29-30; 2:8-14)

Bible Commentary

God's power and provision helps us in our work.

Table of Contents

- Nehemiah - A Positive Role Model
- Hope and Help in God's Provision
    - We Can Seek Guidance About Provision From God...
    - We Are Meant to Depend on God for Provision...
    - We Are Meant to Work Diligently and Wisely...
    - God Does Not Promise That Christians Will Escape the Effects of the Fallen World
    - Wealth is No Indication of God's Favor or Blessing
    - The Final Hope
- Conclusions

Wealth (Mark 10:17-22)

Every resource on our site was made possible through the financial support of people like you. With your gift of any size, you'll enable us to continue equipping Christians with high-quality biblically-based content.

Bookstore

Provision and Wealth Bible Study

God has commissioned us to work and create, to develop the resources he has given us and share with those in need. But what does that look like practically? This topical nine-session Bible study contains tips and encouragement to live a life of generosity and fruitfulness, helping us to redeem our use of resources by nurturing biblical attitudes.

MIX
Papier aus verantwortungsvollen Quellen
Paper from responsible sources
FSC® C105338

Printed by Books on Demand GmbH, Norderstedt / Germany